# TORONTO-HEATHROW

*Half-title:*
**Towing the aircraft to the gate in preparation for the evening flight. . .**

*Title page, top:*
**Before Start checks.**

*Title page, bottom:*
**The flightdeck.** *Boeing*

SEAT MUST BE
IN FORWARD 7 INCHES OF TRAVEL
DURING TAKEOFF AND LANDING

# TORONTO-HEATHROW

## BRUCE CAMPION-SMITH

IAN ALLAN Publishing

First published 1995

ISBN  0 7110 2212 7 (UK)
ISBN 155068-088-9 (Canada)

Published by Ian Allan Publishing: an imprint of Ian Allan Ltd, Terminal House, Station Approach, Shepperton, Surrey TW17 8AS; and printed by Ian Allan Printing Ltd, Coombelands House, Coombelands Lane, Addlestone, Surrey KT15 1HY.

Published in Canada by Vanwell Publishing Limited St. Catharines, Ontario.

# Contents

**An Air Canada Boeing 747-400 landing at Toronto's Pearson International Airport.** *Air Canada*

# Acknowledgements

A book of this nature cannot be written without the support of the airline and this was certainly the case with Air Canada. Staff throughout the airline gave their enthusiastic co-operation from day one.

Capt Wayne MacLellan, Air Canada's vice-president of flight operations, gave his blessing to the project and staff in his office made the arrangements for me to ride on the flightdeck.

I am indebted to Capt Bob Yorke and First Officer Don Boyd who piloted the flight that was the subject of this book. I had the pleasure of joining the two pilots on several other flights as well to familiarise myself with the aircraft's operation. On each flight, they answered my questions, explained procedures and patiently put up with my notebooks, camera and tape recorder.

I must also thank both pilots as well as Capt Bob Thompson, check pilot on the 747-400, for taking the time to review the manuscript and catching some of my gaffes. Any mistakes that remain are, of course, my own.

Mention must be made of Capt Barney Stephanson and First Officer Bill Dyck who permitted me to ride in their company on a flight to Vancouver.

I would also like to extend a word of thanks to the flight attendants for their kind assistance and sharing their expertise. Air Canada's well-deserved reputation for in-flight service is due in large measure to their efforts.

The staff in Air Canada's corporate communications department provided invaluable assistance during the project. Thanks to Denis Couture, the department's former director, whose help enabled the project to get off the ground; and to Ronald White, and Kym Robertson.

Other Air Canada staff who assisted include Bob Tudor, who so kindly escorted me around the ramp at Toronto's Terminal 2 one evening; Tony Coleman and his staff for their help in London; and Pierre Belleau, flight operations support manager.

The maps reproduced in the book were produced by Air Canada's aeronautical services department. L. Grant Wilson, the department's manager, compiled the maps and charts covering the flight's route.

Thanks also to Brian Losito, of Air Canada's audio visual department, for providing the file shots that appear in the book.

Earle Snow, general manager of Gander Area Control Centre, and Brian Bowers, manager of ATC operations in the centre, were generous with their time in explaining the oceanic procedures. It is to the credit of controllers and radio operators on both sides of the ocean that transatlantic flights run so smoothly day after day.

Special mention must be made of John Wheeler and Dean Tougas, both of Boeing's public affairs department, for their help in supplying pictures, manuals and making arrangements for a fascinating tour of the place where jumbo jets are born.

Thanks also to Charles MacColl for some legal advice. And finally, many thanks to Lori who somehow never doubted the project would fly.

One note about the illustrations: it is impossible to photograph a flight like this in one outing. In order to obtain the pictures required to illustrate the text it was necessary to take some of the exterior shots at other times. The photographs were taken by the author unless otherwise noted.

Aviation is ever-changing and that's certainly the case here. Since the pictures were taken for this book, Air Canada has introduced a striking new livery for its fleet: aircraft are white with the trademark red maple leaf set on a dark green tail.

As well, Air Canada has re-configured some of its aircraft, doing away with first class and introducing an upgraded business class service called Executive First. This is located in the forward cabin of the 747-400.

*Bruce Campion Smith*
Toronto
June 1995

*Front cover, top:*
**Air Canada Boeing 747-400.** *Aviation Picture Library*

*Front cover, bottom left:*
**The CN Tower, Toronto.** *Air Canada*

*Front cover, bottom right:*
**The Houses of Parliament.** *Nick Lerwill*

*Back cover:*
**The front end.** *All photographs by the author unless otherwise indicated.*

*Back cover inset:*
**Taxiing.**

# Glossary

| | |
|---|---|
| ACARS | Aircraft Communication Addressing and Reporting System |
| ADF | Automatic Direction Finder |
| ADI | Attitude Director Indicator |
| AFCS | Auto-flight Control System |
| AFDS | Auto-pilot Flight Director System |
| A/P | Auto-pilot |
| A/T | Auto-throttle |
| APP | Approach (auto-pilot mode) |
| APU | Auxiliary Power Unit |
| ASI | Airspeed Indicator |
| ATC | Air Traffic Control |
| ATIS | Automatic Terminal Information Service |
| C of G | Centre of Gravity |
| CAT | Clear Air Turbulence |
| CAT I, II, III | Categories of ILS systems |
| CAVOK | Ceiling and Visibility Okay |
| CDU | Control and Display Unit |
| CMC | Central Maintenance Computer |
| CRT | Cathode Ray Tube |
| Cu | Cumulus cloud |
| DH | Decision Height |
| DME | Distance Measuring Equipment |
| EFIS | Electronic Flight Information System |
| EICAS | Engine Indicating and Crew Alerting System |
| EPR | Engine Pressure Ratio |
| ETA | Expected Time of Arrival |
| FL | Flight level |
| FL CH | Flight Level Change (auto-pilot mode) |
| FMC | Flight Management Computer |
| FMS | Flight Management System |
| F/O | First Officer |
| GPU | Ground Power Unit |
| GS | Glide Slope |
| HF | High Frequency |
| HDG | Heading (auto-pilot mode) |
| IAF | Initial Approach Fix |
| IAS | Indicated Airspeed |
| IFR | Instrument Flight Rules |
| ILS | Instrument Landing System |
| IMC | Instrument Meteorological Conditions |
| INS | Inertial Navigation System |
| IRS | Inertial Reference System |
| kg | Kilogram |
| LNAV | Lateral Navigation (auto-pilot mode) |
| MDA | Minimum Descent Altitude |
| MNPS | Minimum Navigation Performance Sector |
| NAT | North Atlantic |
| ND | Navigation Display |
| NDB | Non-Directional Beacon |
| N1, N2, N3 | Engine compressor speeds expressed as a percentage |
| nm | Nautical mile |
| OCA | Oceanic Control Area |
| PAPA | Parallax Aircraft Parking Aid |
| PFD | Primary Flight Display |
| PIREP | Pilot Report |
| R/T | Radiotelephony |
| RTO | Rejected Take-off |
| RVR | Runway Visual Range |
| SID | Standard Instrument Departure |
| STAR | Standard Terminal Arrival Route |
| TAS | True airspeed |
| UTC | Universal Time Co-ordinated |
| V1 | Take-off decision speed |
| V2 | Take-off safety speed |
| VR | Rotation speed |
| Vref | Reference landing speed |
| VFR | Visual Flight Rules |
| VHF | Very High Frequency (radio) |
| VNAV | Vertical Navigation (auto-pilot mode) |
| VOR | VHF Omni Directional radio range |
| VSI | Vertical Speed Indicator |
| ZFW | Zero Fuel Weight |
| Zulu (Z) | Universal Time Co-ordinated |

# Introduction

They appear first as specks in the distant sky, landing lights twinkling in the afternoon haze. Wearing the colours of Air Canada, British Airways, KLM, Lufthansa and Air France, the Boeing 747s, 767s and DC-10s descend with gear and flaps extended. One by one, they touch down with a squeal of tyres and a burst of blue smoke, ending a journey that began half a world away.

The arrival of the 'big jets' marks the start of the afternoon and evening rush at Toronto's Lester B. Pearson International Airport. Each weekday around 3pm the pace picks up and continues unabated until 9pm with a flurry of domestic, United States and international flights. The ramps surrounding the airport's three terminals are a hub of activity as aircraft are re-fuelled, cabins groomed, galleys stocked, cargo loaded and passengers boarded.

Since aircraft do not make money sitting on the ground, the big jets do not linger long. Within hours of their arrival, they are on the move again, taxiing to the runways and departing for far-off airports, mixed in with short and medium haul jets and turboprop traffic bound for less distant destinations.

One of those flights is Air Canada 856. Each evening it departs Pearson for London's Heathrow airport where it arrives in the early morning after a flight of 6hr 40min. The aircraft used on the route is the Boeing 747-400, a remarkable redesign of the jumbo jet that was first rolled out in 1968. While retaining the familiar shape of the 747, the -400 model is a sophisticated pedigree thanks to advances in aerodynamics, avionics and interior design.

Air Canada uses Boeing 747-400 'Combis', so-called because they can carry a combination of passengers and cargo on the main deck. In addition to the 6,085cu ft of cargo space in forward and aft lower cargo compartments, the 747-400 Combi has room for seven pallets in the rear main deck compartment. A large 134in x 120in (3.4m x 3.0m) main deck door behind the left wing expedites loading and enables ground crews to move cargo at the same time as passengers are boarding in the forward section. In the rear cargo section, roller tracks installed in the floor have taken the place of seats to facilitate the loading and unloading of cargo pallets. The forward and upper deck passenger compartments can carry a total of 277 travellers: 16 in First Class, 50 in Executive Class, and 211 in Hospitality Class. (The actual configuration and passenger capacity can vary.) The cargo and passenger compartments are separated by a partition that is accessible only by crew members. In fact, most passengers are unaware that they are sharing the main deck with a load of cargo! Air Canada's first 747-400 entered service in the spring of 1992 and the airline now has three of the jets flying high density routes across the Atlantic and Pacific.

Britain has long held a special attraction for Canadians. This is probably because so many of them have British ancestry and they live in a country where many of the traditions have British roots. So it's no surprise then that the Toronto-Heathrow flight is a popular one for business travellers and tourists alike, particularly in the summer months when Canadians cross the ocean by the thousands to visit relatives and tour the sights. And with three or four scheduled carriers and a handful of charter outfits flying Toronto-Britain, there's no shortage of airlines willing to fly them there!

Nowadays, flights across the Atlantic are accepted as routine by the thousands of passengers who make the crossing each day. Yet this has not always been the case; for years the weather and sheer length of the over-water legs presented a huge obstacle to air travel across the ocean. Air Canada's transatlantic service dates back to 1943, a time when ocean flying was still very much in its infancy, when the Canadian Government created the Canadian Government Transatlantic Air Service. This wartime measure was put in place to provide a fast and regular mail service to Canadian troops stationed in Britain and to transport diplomatic passengers. Trans-Canada Air Lines, the forerunner of Air Canada, was chosen to operate the flights.

An Avro Lancaster bomber was hastily converted for the job at hand and dubbed the Lancastrian for airline service. The gun turrets in the nose and tail were removed and replaced by streamlined cones and a large auxiliary fuel tank was installed in the bomb bay to give the aircraft the range needed to span the Atlantic. Eight to 10 seats were also fitted in the fuselage to accommo-

date the passengers but no amount of modifications could hide the fact that the Lancaster was built for bombing and not for comfort. Government officials originally wanted to use four C-54s, the military version of the DC-4 airliner. However, such aircraft were in short supply and high demand and none could be obtained, so additional Lancasters were modified and put in service.

The first flight on 23 July 1943, between Montreal, Quebec, and Prestwick, Scotland, carried 2,600lb of mail and three passengers. The journey took 12hr 25min and set a new record for the crossing. By the end of 1945, a total of nine Lancastrians had completed more than 500 crossings and carried 1.5 million pounds of mail. The flights enabled TCA crews to hone their skills in Atlantic flying and the challenges of weather and navigation that went with it. In 1946, the route was extended to London and the service took on more of the styling of a civilian airline with the introduction of the North Star, a Canadian version of the DC-4. In the years since, other Air Canada aircraft on the Toronto-London route have included Super Constellations, DC-8s, L-1011s, 767s and now Boeing 747-400s.

**Trans-Canada Air Lines, the forerunner of Air Canada, used the civilian version of the Lancaster bomber for early transatlantic flights.** *Air Canada*

This book will take readers behind the scenes of Air Canada flight 856 to Heathrow. The flight attendants and pilots on a transatlantic flight are the most visible players in an effort that involves the work of literally hundreds and even thousands of people behind the scenes: the reservations agent who sold a ticket on the flight several months ago; the team of cooks who prepared the meals; the air traffic controllers who will safely guide the aircraft on its long journey; and the airline staff who tend to the planes on the ground. These days, the sophistication and safety of modern aircraft and the exacting training of the crews that fly them have made such journeys routine — a far cry from those first noisy, cold and arduous crossings in the Lancastrian!

**Boeing 747-400 C-GAGM sporting the smart new Air Canada livery is seen on final approach to Heathrow.** *Peter R. March*

# Flightdeck

Once a week, sometime around midnight, the massive blue hangar doors of a Boeing factory rumble open, spilling light on to the darkened ramp as a glistening new 747-400 is pulled out into the cool, damp air. It's an event that happens four or five times a month at the plant in Everett, Washington, which is best known as the birthplace of jumbo jets — the home of Boeing 747s.

The new 747-400 is towed to one of the paint shops where it spends the next four days being transformed from an anonymous shell into a flying billboard for the carrier that will fly it. It is then fuelled and towed on to the flightline where it undergoes three weeks of final work, system tests and inspections. Then it's time for the new jet to try its wings during three to five flight tests.

Once everything checks out okay, one of the world's airlines will take delivery of its new aircraft and another venerable jumbo will begin plying the long-haul routes across the globe.

A quarter century has passed since Boeing first introduced the jumbo jet to the world's wonder. Looking back, the 747 seemed like a natural progression in commercial aviation yet, at the time, the project represented a huge financial gamble for the company. Boeing did not even have a factory big enough to build its proposed new aircraft. A sprawling plant was built on a 780-acre parcel of land adjoining Paine Field in Everett and production of the first 747s started as the final phases of the building were completed. Already the largest building in the world by volume, the main assembly area has continued to grow. It was expanded by 45% in 1979 and 1980 to house the 767 line and most recently enlarged another 50% — from 25 to 39 hectares — to accommodate the production line for the Boeing 777 twin-jet.

A legion of jumbos have followed that first 747 out of those big, blue factory doors: the original -100 model; Combis that carry cargo and passengers on the main deck; Freighters dedicated solely to cargo; the stubby, long-range 747SP (Special Performance); the 550-seat 747SR (Short Range); the -200 series that became the mainstay of the 747 line; and the -300 series which introduced the stretched upper deck.

Those 747 models bridged most continents but could not reliably offer non-stop services on the lucrative Pacific routes such as New York-Tokyo and Los Angeles-Sydney. Strong headwinds could stretch a flight beyond a jet's endurance, forcing stop-overs in Anchorage or Honolulu to refuel. Reacting to growing demand from airlines, Boeing began design work in early 1984 on an aircraft that could cross the Pacific non-stop, year-round — even on days when the strong westerly headwinds slowed flights. The aircraft that emerged from the planners' drawing boards and computer screens was the 747-400, a dramatic overhaul of the 747. Northwest Airlines was the launch customer, placing an order for 10 of the new aircraft in the autumn of 1985 and Boeing went to work. The first -400 model rolled out in January 1988.

From the outside, there's little to distinguish the -400 model from its predecessors. It shares the same enlarged upper deck of the 747-300 (double the size of the -200 series) and its length and height are the same: 232ft nose to tail and 63.5ft from the ground to the top of the tail, about the height of a six-storey building. One aerodynamic improvement, however, is quickly apparent — the -400's wings have been stretched six feet and have sprung winglets. Angled upward and slightly outward, the 6ft high winglets improve the efficiency of the wing by reducing the powerful vortices that form at the wingtips. On all aircraft, high pressure air from beneath the wing wraps around the wingtip and mixes with the lower pressure on top, producing strong vortices that trail behind and create drag. Because vortices are a by-product of lift, they can never be completely eliminated. But the winglets, made from graphite and epoxy composite materials and aluminium, reduce the strength of the vortices, resulting in less drag and a two per cent saving in fuel burn.

There are other improvements incorporated into the 747-400 as well: a new 12,490 litre fuel tank in the tail assembly boosts the aircraft's range by 350nm; carbon brakes, like those offered on the 757 and 767, are standard on the -400 and offer better heat and wear resistance. Powerplant and design improvements have raised the take-off weight from 710,000lb for the 747-100 to 870,000lb for the -400 and range has gone from 4,600nm to 7,360nm.

But the most dramatic change in the 747-400 is the totally electronic flightdeck. The dozens of dials, switches and instruments that competed for space in the older cockpit have been replaced by six large cathode ray tubes that display all the

The dramatic advances of the 747-400's flightdeck are quickly apparent when compared to the earlier 747 cockpit. Flight, navigation and engine information on the -400 is presented to the pilots on six large CRTs, eliminating the clutter of instrumentation found in earlier 747 cockpits. In front of each pilot is a Primary Flight Display (PFD) and a Navigation Display (ND). Two Engine Indications and Crew Alerting System (EICAS) displays are located in the centre of the instrument panel for easy viewing by both pilots. *Boeing (both)*

information the pilots require. The two-crew glass cockpit builds on the design pioneered in the 757 and 767 jets and goes even further by virtually eliminating the traditional flight instruments, like the airspeed indicator and altimeter. In fact, the number of flightdeck lights, gauges and switches has been reduced from 971 to 365, 19 fewer than the 757/767 and remarkably, 100 less than the twin-jet 737!

The redesign means that the flight engineer required on earlier 747s has gone the way of the navigator and the task of monitoring the jet's many systems has, for the most part, been automated. The instrumentation for the aircraft systems, which took up the whole side wall of the flight engineer's station, has been greatly simplified and incorporated into the overhead panel within easy reach of the pilots. The result is a futuristic, uncluttered, flightdeck that has dramatically cut pilot workload and stress and enabled two pilots to safely and efficiently fly a four-engine aircraft.

The upper deck and flightdeck are accessed by a straight staircase (gone is the spiral staircase on the early models) located just opposite door two on the port side. With the flight engineer's station and the accompanying mass of instrumentation now gone, the flightdeck appears more spacious than the older cockpits but is still surprisingly cosy, given the size of the jumbo. Yet, the space is perfect for the job at hand with careful consideration given for the needs of the crew, right down to spots for stowing charts and flightbags. From their perch some three storeys above the tarmac, the pilots really have no sense of the tremendous size of the aircraft that is behind them. From the side windows, they can just see the outer portion of each wing, including the outboard engines, although from this vantage point, it's hard to believe that the distant winglets are man-sized. With the seats pulled forward, the crew have a good view ahead over the glareshield.

All the instrumentation required to fly and navigate the aircraft is presented on eight-inch square CRTs, called the Primary Flight Display (PFD) and Navigation Display (ND) located on the front instrument panel. Because they are larger, the CRTs on the -400 are situated side by side in front of the pilots, unlike the smaller CRTs on the 757/767 which are located one on top of the other.

The PFD is located directly in front of each pilot and incorporates the basic 'T' instruments on one screen for easy viewing. The bulk of the PFD is dominated by a computer-generated Attitude Director Indicator (ADI) that displays flight attitude, ILS signals and flight director commands. The selected ILS frequency and DME read-out are shown on the upper left and radio altimeter read-outs and decision height are on the upper right.

The Primary Flight Display (PFD) incorporates the basic 'T' flight information on one display for easy scanning. In the centre is the attitude director. Airspeed is shown on the left, altitude on the right and a partial compass rose on the bottom. In this example, the PFD shows an ILS approach to Heathrow's Runway 27 Right. The jet is stabilised on the glideslope and localiser, passing 2,700ft at 161kt and descending at 1,000ft/min. The centre autopilot is in control of the aircraft as indicated by CMD. The hash marks on the attitude director show the pitch attitude that should be flown if the jet encounters windshear. The diamonds on the right and bottom of the attitude director show the ILS raw data signals.

On either side of the ADI, vertical tape displays show airspeed, altitude and vertical speed. Located on the left, the airspeed tape shows the airspeed in 10kt increments, highlighting the current speed as it scrolls through a pointer box. Important speeds, such as flap retraction speeds and V-speeds for take-off, are marked on the airspeed tape in various colours. The tape display on the right side shows the altitude with the alert or selected altitudes shown at the top of the scale and the altimeter setting at the bottom. The vertical speed is displayed by a pointer right of the altimeter with the exact rate shown above the display in a climb and below it during a descent. Heading information is presented on a compass

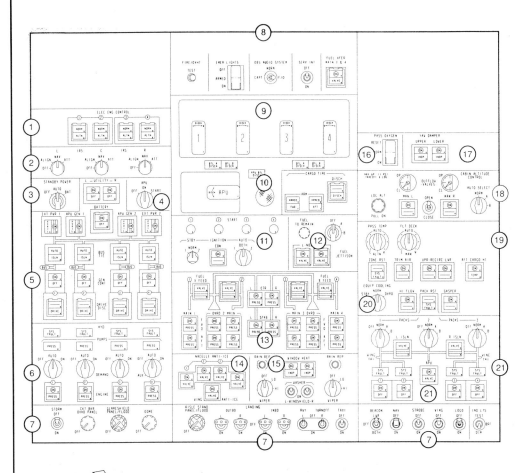

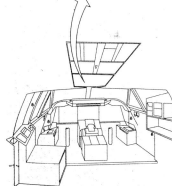

1. Electronic engine control
2. Inertial reference system mode select
3. Standby power
4. Auxiliary power unit
5. Electrical system
6. Hydraulic system
7. Lighting
8. Miscellaneous controls
9. Fire control panel
10. Voice recorder area microphone
11. Engine start
12. Fuel jettison
13. Fuel management panel
14. Nacelle/wing anti-ice
15. Windshield wipers/window heat
16. Passenger oxygen
17. Yaw damper
18. Cabin altitude
19. Temperature controls
20. Equipment cooling
21. Bleed air system

**The overhead panel.** *Boeing*

arc at the base of the display and auto-throttle and navigation mode indications are located across the top.

The Navigation Displays are located inboard of the PFDs and present navigation information in a variety of formats — MAP, PLAN, VOR and ILS as well as familiar depiction of an HSI for VOR, ILS and ADF navigation. Typically, the ND is left in MAP mode which depicts 80° of compass rose across the top of the display with the jet's current heading highlighted in a box. Below that is a moving map display showing the flight-planned waypoints with the aircraft position marked at the base of the screen by a white triangle. The large screens allows the crew to select ranges from 10nm for navigation during departure and arrival and up to 640nm for *en route* navigation. Wind direction and strength is continuously displayed in the upper left corner and the ETA and distance to the next waypoint is shown in the upper right corner.

At the touch of a button, the pilots can call up a host of other information on the ND such as the location of airports and radio beacons. As well,

the read-out from the weather radar can be overlaid the route to help pilots pick their way around severe weather.

The EICAS (Engine Indicating and Crew Alerting System) is located on two CRTs in the centre of the instrument panel, one above the other. The system displays engine indications, a variety of maintenance data and system status information and a central crew alerting system with colour-coded alert messages. These replace the bewildering array of engine dials that crowded the centre panel on previous 747s.

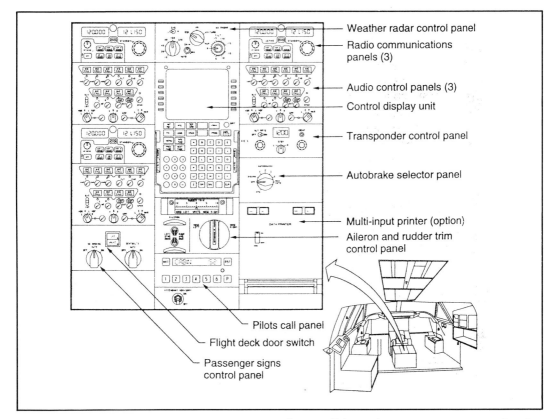

- Weather radar control panel
- Radio communications panels (3)
- Audio control panels (3)
- Control display unit
- Transponder control panel
- Autobrake selector panel
- Multi-input printer (option)
- Aileron and rudder trim control panel
- Pilots call panel
- Flight deck door switch
- Passenger signs control panel

**Diagram of the centre panel.** *Boeing*

The top CRT is normally used to display the three primary engine indications: engine pressure ratio (EPR), N1 fan speed and the exhaust gas temperature (EGT) as well as crew alerting messages, fuel quantity and environmental control system information. Gear and flap indications are at the bottom right and appear only when the gear or flaps are down or are in transit. Engine parameters are presented on vertical scale tapes, rather than the dial format found on the 757/767.

The systems on the -400 have been designed on the 'dark cockpit' concept meaning that they need attention only when there is a problem or pilot action is required. The crew alerting function continuously monitors all aircraft systems and displays a message on the upper CRT if a fault occurs. The messages are divided into several categories: warnings alert the pilots to operational or system conditions that could endanger the aircraft, like an engine fire. Warning messages are displayed in red at the top of the EICAS message and are accompanied by the master warning lights on the glareshield and an aural alert, such as a voice, bell or siren. Caution messages are shown

for conditions that are not emergencies but require action by the crew, such as low oil pressure. These are displayed in amber below the warning messages and activate the master caution lights and a beeper that sounds four times in one second. To prevent a distraction during the take-

**The thrust levers are located close at hand on the centre console. The speed-brake lever is to the left of the throttles and the flap lever is on the right. The fuel controls are located behind the thrust levers. The small parking brake lever is visible on the left.**

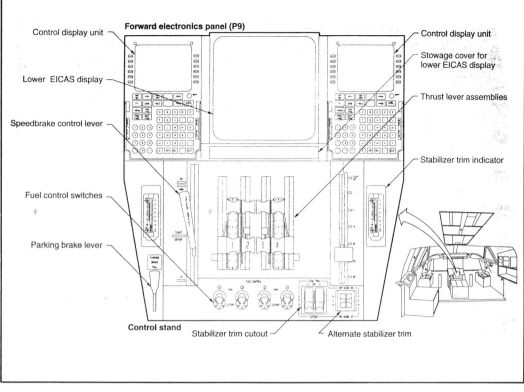

Forward electronics panel (P9)

Control display unit

Lower EICAS display

Speedbrake control lever

Fuel control switches

Parking brake lever

Control display unit

Stowage cover for lower EICAS display

Thrust lever assemblies

Stabilizer trim indicator

**Control stand**

Stabilizer trim cutout

Alternate stabilizer trim

**The forward electronics panel and throttles.** *Boeing*

off roll, some of the warnings and cautions are inhibited until after the aircraft is safely airborne. Advisories, also shown in amber, are conditions that the crew should be aware of. Memos are reminders to the crew about the status of certain manually selected normal conditions, such as the selection of the no smoking sign or parking brake. They are displayed in white at the bottom of the message field.

The lower CRT is used to present secondary engine information, such as N2 compressor speeds and oil temperature and pressures. The pilots can also, at the touch of a button, call up system diagrams on the screen to show the configuration of any one of the six major aircraft systems: doors, electrical, fuel, environmental, gear and hydraulic. These displays are chosen from a selector located on the right side of the glareshield and can tell the pilots a variety of information, including the temperature throughout the cabin, the pressure of the tyres and status of fuel pumps and valves.

To guard against the loss of information in the event of a failure, each CRT is able to display the

PFD, ND or EICAS display. The display system automatically transfers the PFD to the inboard CRT if it detects a failure of the outboard CRT or will transfer the main EICAS to the lower screen

Control panels for the PFD and ND are located at each end of the glareshield. The knobs on top are used to set MDA and altimeter setting and the selectors below change the ND mode and range. The six buttons across the bottom are used to select additional information on the ND such as weather radar and airport locations. On the left are the buttons used to call up various synoptics on the EICAS displays.

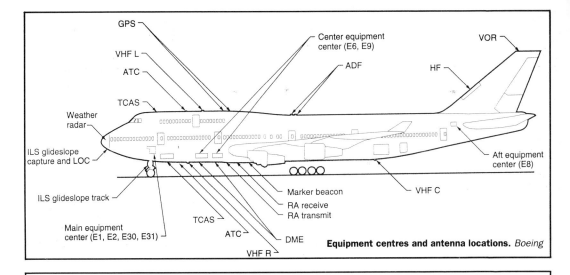

GPS

VHF L

ATC

TCAS

Weather radar

ILS glideslope capture and LOC

ILS glideslope track

Main equipment center (E1, E2, E30, E31)

TCAS

ATC

VHF R

Center equipment center (E6, E9)

ADF

VOR

HF

Marker beacon

RA receive

RA transmit

DME

VHF C

Aft equipment center (E8)

**Equipment centres and antenna locations.** *Boeing*

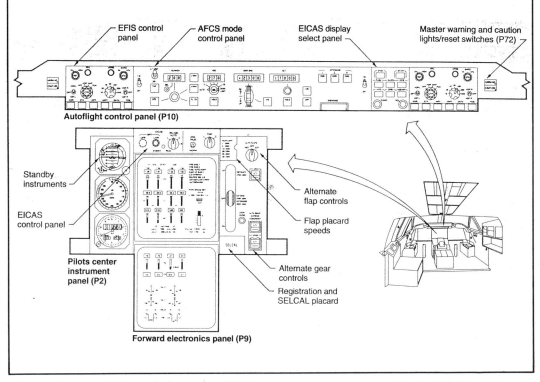

EFIS control panel

AFCS mode control panel

EICAS display select panel

Master warning and caution lights/reset switches (P72)

**Autoflight control panel (P10)**

Standby instruments

EICAS control panel

**Pilots center instrument panel (P2)**

Alternate flap controls

Flap placard speeds

Alternate gear controls

Registration and SELCAL placard

**Forward electronics panel (P9)**

**The centre instrument panel and auto-flight control panel.** *Boeing*

when it detects a failure of the upper CRT. As well, the pilots can manually transfer a function to another CRT using controls located above each set of displays. For instance, the EICAS or PFD can be selected on the inboard CRT.

Though the electronic displays have proven to be extremely reliable in service, three mechanical standby instruments for attitude, airspeed indicator and altimeter are located to the right of the captain's ND and a radio magnetic indicator, used for tracking VORs and NDBs, is located to the left of the PFD. At each end of the glareshield, control panels for the Electronic Flight Instrument System (EFIS) enable each pilot to adjust the brightness of the displays.

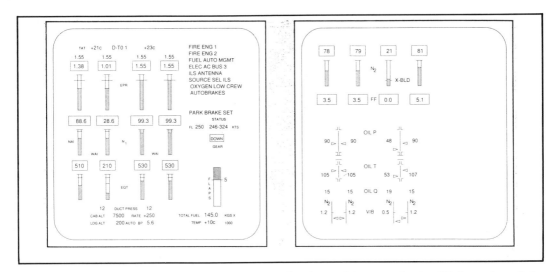

**Main and auxiliary EICAS display.** *Boeing*

The console between the two pilots contains the thrust levers with the speed brake on the left side and the flap lever on the right. Behind that is located the usual assortment of selection panels for the VHF radios, weather radar, HF tuners and transponder. Noticeably absent are the VOR and ADF tuners. The VOR receivers are normally auto-tuned by the FMC but can be manually tuned through the control display units (CDU) as well as the ADF receivers. To the right of the EICAS displays are the landing gear selector handle and alternate flap and gear controls. Above, the over-head panel is a much simplified version of the flight engineer's panel with controls for the fuel, electrical and hydraulic systems as well as pressurisation, bleed air, APU and IRS. The panel also contains the switches for exterior lights, windshield wipers and anti-icing.

The electronic brain of the aircraft is the Flight Management Computer System. The FMC is accessed through two CDUs located at the front of

**The PFD and ND during cruise over the Atlantic. The small circle on the ND marks the location of the airport at Shannon, Ireland.**

the centre console and as soon will be seen, much of the control of the aircraft is done through the computer. Relying on flight plan information input by the crew, data drawn from onboard systems and information from an extensive navigation database, the FMC computes the optimum flight profile that balances speed and economy. The computer calculates optimum-cost flight profiles for climb, cruise and descent and supplies commands to the auto-pilot and auto-throttle during automatic flight. If the aircraft is being flown manually, the FMC can supply commands to the flight director so the pilots can follow the computed path.

The FMC navigational database contains information on VORs, including frequencies and identifiers, waypoints, airways, airports, runways, SIDs and STARs. At the push of a few buttons, the pilots can tell their track and distance from virtually any radio beacon, intersection or airport in the world. The FMC will even display the message 'Insufficient Fuel' if the programmed destination is out of range. The database is updated every 28 days and is capable of storing one million words of data. During a flight, the FMC searches the navigational database and automatically selects the two best DME signals which it uses in conjunction with the IRS position data to compute the jet's position. If the aircraft is out of range of VHF signals, the FMS navigates using the IRS alone.

The computer also holds a performance database containing the aerodynamics model of the aircraft as well as data on fuel flow, engine thrust and N1 limits. This information is used by the FMC to calculate optimum profile and speeds for climb, cruise and descent.

A third CDU located at the rear of the centre console is used by pilots for ACARS, the Aircraft Communication Addressing and Reporting System. This data-link system sends information between aircraft and an airline ground base, allowing pilots easy communications for dispatch and weather updates. Using the keyboard, the pilots type in messages which are then transmitted to airline operations staff, air traffic control or even other aircraft in the fleet. As well, ACARS automatically transmits out of gate, off the ground and on the gate times to keep airline dispatchers up-to-date on flight progress.

The Central Maintenance Computer System is also accessed through the rear CDU. The CMC continuously monitors all the major avionics, electrical and electro-mechanical systems and provides easy central access to maintenance data for all aircraft systems. Through a central menu page, pilots and technicians are able to call up present leg faults, existing faults and fault history on various aircraft systems, such as fuel, electrical, flight control and hydraulic. Remarkably, the aircraft has the ability to troubleshoot itself and report problems to technicians, making the complex aircraft very user-friendly. Two maintenance computers provide backup in case one fails. Approximately 7,800 fault messages may be generated and up to 500 faults stored in the CMC memory. If required, the maintenance data can be sent via ACARS to airline technicians on the ground. With this advance notice, the technicians can be ready to make necessary repairs upon the aircraft's arrival.

The level of automation designed into the -400 saves the pilots from the more tedious chores and allows them to devote their attention to the important tasks of managing the flight and thinking ahead. But as will soon be seen, there is no shortage of work for the pilots.

**The test aircraft in flight.** *Boeing*

# Pre-Flight

It's early evening and the international wing of Terminal 2 at Toronto's Pearson International Airport is crowded with passengers and their mounds of luggage. Outside the check-in area, groups of travellers spend a final few moments with friends and relatives, snapping some photographs, shedding some tears and saying goodbye.

Capt Bob Yorke and First Officer Don Boyd arrive at the terminal building for an evening flight and ease their way through the crowds. On this June day, they will be piloting Air Canada 856, a six-and-a-half hour journey across the Atlantic Ocean to London's Heathrow Airport. The jet for today's flight is the Boeing 747-400 Combi, one of the newest members of the 747 family. It's a beautiful night for the trip; the clouds that had blanketed the city for much of the day have given way to a clear sky with only a few puffy cumulus clouds dotting the horizon.

First stop for the two pilots is Air Canada's Flight Operations office at the east end of the terminal, located conveniently near the international check-in. It's here, in this third floor office, that the pilots pick up the paperwork and begin the pre-flight planning for the trip ahead. The pilots usually arrive at the airport about 60-90min before their flight to allow plenty of time to go over the flightplan and prepare the aircraft. On this day, however, both Bob and Don were called at home by crew scheduling staff and told to come in a bit later than usual because of a delay on the flight. Arriving at the Flight Operations office, they find out the reason for the delay. A Boeing 747 'Classic', an affectionate term referring to older models of the 747, was scheduled to fly a return trip to Kingston, Jamaica, earlier in the day but suffered a mechanical problem. One of the airline's -400s was pressed into service for the flight. The aircraft has only just returned to Toronto and the ground crews need time to turn it around for the transatlantic run. The result is that Air Canada 856, originally scheduled to depart at 19.50 will now leave at 20.30 local time or 0030 Universal Time Co-ordinated (UTC). To eliminate confusion, the aviation world operates on one time, known as UTC or Zulu time; all time references in the book will be UTC.

Bob and Don take a few moments to pick up their mail, look over the company memos on the bulletin boards and chat with a few of the many pilots in the busy office. The crew then retrieve the paperwork for the day's flight from a large file and spread it out on a nearby counter. The flightplans are prepared by an Air Canada dispatcher in Toronto. But the ultimate responsibility for the aircraft and the passengers rests with the flightcrew so they give the paperwork a thorough

**Capt Bob Yorke and First Officer Don Boyd review the flightplan.**

```
QU YYZOPAC YYZWAAC
.YYZOAAC 302259
FUEL ADJUSTED  3 PERCENT ACCT ABOVE AVG CONSUMPTION ACFT 342

FP  856/30 B747 342 C/GAGM SEL/DPKQ M860 CAPT RS YORKE

RMKS/     SEE VCI FLT PLAN TO PICKUP 10MINS..PLEASE ADZ FLT DISP
COMMENTS RE VCI

CYYZ 0030Z YYZ078R/J594 MSS J586 YJN J500 YSC DRCT MIILS NA67
 FROSS DRCT DOTTY TRACK VICTOR BEL UB3 HON DRCT WCO DRCT BNN DRCT
 EGLL

ALTN EGPF MAX OCA F390 G/C 3080
```

| TO | EET ET/AT F/L | M/T | T/T | DST | TAS | TDV | WIND | COMP | TR/SH | MFOB |
|---|---|---|---|---|---|---|---|---|---|---|
| MSS | 0031.../..330 | | | 223 | 509 | P08 | 30062 | P032 | 41/01 | 65.6 |
| MIILS | 0107.../..330 | | | 346 | 506 | P06 | 27075 | P061 | 41/01 | 58.2 |
| FROSS | 0133.../..370 | | | 247 | 502 | P08 | 24075 | P072 | 34/02 | 53.6 |
| DOTTY | 0200.../..370 | | | 266 | 500 | P06 | 23084 | P084 | 36/03 | 48.8 |
| 52N 50W | 0223.../..370 | 093 | 069 | 225 | 497 | P04 | 23093 | P089 | 36/03 | 44.8 |
| 54N 40W | 0302.../..370 | 096 | 072 | 380 | 496 | P03 | 24091 | P090 | 36/02 | 38.1 |
| 55N 30W | 0339.../..370 | 101 | 080 | 353 | 494 | P01 | 27089 | P088 | 36/02 | 31.9 |
| 55N 20W | 0416.../..390 | 107 | 090 | 344 | 493 | STD | 28062 | P061 | 36/03 | 26.0 |
| 55N 10W | 0454.../..390 | 102 | 090 | 344 | 492 | M01 | 28045 | P045 | 36/01 | 19.9 |
| BEL | 0509.../..390 | | | 132 | 491 | M02 | 27025 | P025 | 36/00 | 17.5 |
| IOM | 0517.../..370 | | | 62 | 491 | M02 | 28019 | P018 | 36/00 | 16.4 |
| EGLL | 0558.../..370 | | | 225 | 498 | P04 | 13009 | M004 | 36/00 | 13.5 |

```
               TTL DST 3147 TMP P03   CMP P057
```

| BURN | FIT | ALTN | RF | EROP | TF | TODMF | ELW | DSD |
|---|---|---|---|---|---|---|---|---|
| 62.1 | 4.1 | 9.4 | 3.1 | 0.0 | 1.4 | 14.6 | 255.9 | 100 |

```
LOW FL 330 0554/ 63.9


ALTN EGPF
EGLL SID WOBUN DRCT WELIN UA2 POL UB4 MARGO TRN125R/DCS339R FENIK
 DRCT EGPF
```

| TO | EET | ETA | F/L | DIST | TAS | TDV | WIND | COMP | TR/SH | BURN | MFOB |
|---|---|---|---|---|---|---|---|---|---|---|---|
| EGPF | 0051.......310 | | | 304 | 487 | P01 | 20020 | P012 | 36/02 | 9.4 | 4.1 |

```
EROPS ALTS CYYR/EINN/
```

*Above:*
**Before the flight, the crew pick up their mail and check the bulletin boards for important notices.**

*Left:*
**The flightplan.**

*Below:*
**The First Officer checks actual and forecast weather reports for *en route* and alternate airports and London Heathrow.**

scrutiny and are quick to make changes if necessary. For example, the Captain will often decide to request additional fuel if there is any hint of possible weather or air traffic control delays, especially when flying into a busy airport like Heathrow.

The flightplan lays out the most efficient route for Air Canada 856, taking into account factors like weather, the day's designated tracks across the North Atlantic, take-off weight and particularly winds aloft. The lengthy computer print-out details the exact route, alternate airports to be used in the event that a diversion is necessary, forecast winds, fuel burn for each leg of the trip, preliminary load and weight figures, estimated arrival times at each fix *en route* as well as significant NOTAMS (Notices to Airmen) that could impact the flight.

With upwards of 800 flights a day crossing the North Atlantic, leaving the routeing of each flight to the whims of the individual flight crews would obviously create the potential for a hazardous situation. In order to ensure safety, designated tracks called the Oceanic Track System are developed by the two air traffic control centres responsible for traffic over the North Atlantic. Tracks for eastbound flights are plotted by Gander ATC and westbound tracks selected by their counterparts in Prestwick, Scotland. These tracks organise the flow so controllers can accommodate the maximum number of aircraft in the minimum amount of airspace close to the minimum flying time.

Each day, ATC staff in Gander with the assistance of a computer plot a best time, great circle route from New York's Kennedy airport to London, a route that will suit most European-bound flights from the eastern seaboard. Once one route has been identified as the minimum time track, four to five parallel tracks are plotted around this track, taking into account factors like airspace restrictions or significant weather. The parallel tracks run one degree of latitude, or 60nm, apart and, in the case of eastbound flights, are developed to take advantage of tailwinds or for westbound flights to avoid the worst headwinds. These tracks are published internationally by 1400Z (ie 14.00hrs Zulu) each day and airlines planning a transatlantic crossing then pick the track and flight level that best suits them. Although congestion on the air routes sometimes means that pilots have to settle for their second choice of track or altitude, Gander ATC prides itself on being able to accommodate about 85 per cent of the requests.

Today's routeing will take Air Canada 856 to the coast of Canada via Jet Route 594 to MSS, a VOR at Massena, New York; J586 to YJN, a VOR at St. Jean, Quebec, just south of Montreal; J500 to YSC at Sherbrooke, Quebec; direct MIILS, a waypoint north of Fredericton, New Brunswick;

```
 ;AWDAF/R/YYZLHR                                         93/06/30 23:26
YYZ   FT 302246 2323 /SCT. 13Z 30 SCT C100 BKN /BKN 1010G20. 18Z C25 BKN 100
               BKN /BKN 1010G20 OCNL C15 OVC 4RW-F.
YYZ   SA 302300 40 SCT 100 SCT 300 SCT 25 187/20/11/1708/008/CU1AC1CI1 AC/CI
               TRS 0611
YOW   SA 302300 65 SCT 240 SCT 25 171/23/7/3407/003/CU1CI1 3000
YMX   SA 302300 E50 BKN 100 BKN 270 BKN 45 170/22/12/0607/003/SC6AC1CI1 SHWRS
               N-NE 0067
YUL   SA 302300 55 SCT 70 SCT 260 SCT 45 163/23/11/1105/001/SC3AC1CI1 TCU
               ASOCTD SHWRS N 1944
YQB   SA 302300 45 SCT 90 SCT 30 161/19/13/0706/000/CU1AC1 2011
YZV   SA 302300 12 SCT 20 SCT 110 SCT 250 SCT 30 155/11/9/2105/998/
               SF1SC2AC1CI1 0322
YQM   SA 302300 15 SCT M30 BKN 15 136/15/12/0210/993/CF2SC5 CB S MVG E 2378
YHZ   SA 302300 25 SCT 70 SCT 250 SCT 15 130/20/15/2804/991/TCU1AC1CI1 7522
YQY   SP 302322 10 SCT 20 SCT M70 BKN 250 BKN 15 0000 CF1TCU2AC3CI1
YQY   RS 302300 10 SCT 20 SCT 70 SCT E140 BKN 250 OVC 8TRW-- 100/16/15/
               2504/983/CF2CB2AC1AC3CI1 CB NE MVG E 849X
YJT   SA 302300 5 SCT 15 SCT E40 BKN 10 094/12/10/2516/981/SF2SC3SC4 7999
YQX   SA 302300 M2 BKN 50 OVC 21/2R-F 125/8/8/1312G20/989/ST7SC3 16XX

 ;AWDAF/S/LHR
LHR   FT 302200 0624 03007KT CAVOK PROB30 TEMPO 0608 7000 6ST008 PROB10 TEMPO
               1318 7000 95TS
LHR   FC 302100 2207 10008KT CAVOK PROB30 TEMPO 0307 5000 6ST006
LHR   SA 302300 2250 05004KT CAVOK 19/12 1018 NOSIG
...END
```

```
QU YVROSAC YEGXXAC YYCXXAC YYZOPAC YYZWAAC
.YYZOACC 301609
EASTBOUND NORTH ATLANTIC TRACK
TIME 010100/010800
TRACK U/YAY/5350/5540/5630/5620/5610/MAC
EBND FL/330/350/370/390
NAR095 NAR099 NAR            UK     VIA
TRACK V/DOTTY/5250/5440/5530/5520/5510/BEL
EBND FL/330/350/370/390
NAR081 NAR087 NAR            UK     VIA
TRACK W/CYMON/5150/5340/5430/5420/5415/BABAN
EBND FL/310/330/350/370/390
NAR071 NAR075 NAR            UK     VIA
TRACK X/YQX/5050/5240/5330/5320/5315/BURAK
EBND FL/310/330/350/370/390
NAR061 NAR067 NAR            UK     VIA
TRACK Y/VIXUN/4950/5140/5230/5220/5215/DOLIP
EBND FL/330/350/370/390
NAR051 NAR057 NAR            UK     VIA
TRACK Z/YYT/4850/5040/5130/5120/5115/GIPER
EBND FL/330/350/370/390
NAR041 NAR045 NAR            UK     VIA
 REMARKS:
1. OPERATORS ARE REMINDED THAT SPECIFIC MNPS CERTIFICATION TO
    OPERATE WITHIN MNPS AIRSPACE F275-F400 IS REQD FROM THEIR
    STATE AVIATION AUTHORITY.
2. OPERATORS SHOULD REFER TO NOTAM A1743/C1237/93- ADHERENCE
    TO MACH NUMBER
 ;
  30JUN1610 FLQ 125
```

```
ACFT DEVIATIONS
NIL

CREW ALERTS
NIL


ICAO FLT PLN
 (FPL-ACA856-IS
-B747F/H-SXI/C
-CYYZ0030
-N0497F330 YYZ078R J594 MSS J586 YJN J500 YSC DCT
 MIILS/N0501F350 NA67 FROSS DCT DOTTY/M086F350 NATV
 55N030W/M086F390 55N010W/N0491F390 BEL/N0491F370 UB3 HON DCT
 WCO DCT BNN DCT
-EGLL0558 EGPF
-EET/MSS0031 MIILS0107 FROSS0133 DOTTY0200 50W0223 40W0302
 30W0339 20W0416 10W0454 BEL0509 IOM0517
 REG/CGAGM SEL/DPKQ RMK/H/B747F/R EROPS 180 MIN RULE  AGCS EQUIPPED
 02.V330 03.W370
```

and then North American Route 67 to FROSS, a waypoint over the Gulf of St Lawrence.

The dispatcher has selected Track Victor, one of six tracks plotted by ATC this night, to take advantage of a 100kt jetstream that should help speed the journey. Air Canada 856 will enter the Gander Oceanic Control Area at DOTTY, a waypoint just south of St Anthony, Newfoundland, and will proceed on an easterly heading to 52 North, 50 west, (shortened to 5250N) and on to 5440N, 5530N, 5520N and 5510N. The flight will make landfall over Northern Ireland and from Belfast it will follow the Upper Blue 3 airway to IOM, the VOR on the southern tip of the Isle of Man; on to the Honiley VOR, southeast of Birmingham; direct to WCO, an NDB west of Luton and direct to the Bovingdon VOR, located on the northwest outskirts of London, before making the approach into Heathrow. The flight will cover 3,147nm and Flight Level 330 (FL330), or 33,000ft, is the initial planned altitude.

*Top left:*
**Print-out showing weather reports for Toronto (YYZ) and *en route* airports including Ottawa (YOW), Montreal's Dorval and Mirabel airports (YUL and YMX), Quebec City (YQB), Moncton (YQM), Halifax (YHZ), Gander (YQX) and, of course, Heathrow (LHR).**

*Bottom left:*
**Print-out of the day's eastbound NAT tracks.**

**Flightplan filed with ATC.**

Though the flightplan may resemble an alphabet soup, the letters and numbers are easily deciphered by the pilots and the FMC. Just as highways and roads on the ground have names, so do routings in the sky. Airways above 18,000ft, the transition level between high and low level airspace in Canada and the United States, are called Jet Routes while those below that level are known as Victor Routes. Airports are identified by a four-letter designator, like CYYZ for Toronto and EGLL for London Heathrow, and NDB and VOR radio beacons are typically identified by two or three letters. Intersections and waypoints are labelled with a five-letter identifier, like FROSS, and while they sometimes relate to a nearby geographic point, they can often be nonsensical.

From the NOTAMs, the crew note that X-ray NDB at Toronto is out of service for a short time. In order to get the optimum altitude and route on the NAT, transatlantic crews are requested to call Gander Flight Service with a coast-out fix estimate sent over primary HF frequency 5616 and secondary 2899. The call should include aircraft identification, coast-out fix estimate and maximum acceptable flight level at oceanic boundary. The information is needed 90-120min prior to arriving at the boundary. The notes for Heathrow show that a start-up clearance frequency has been changed, a new high level hold has been established and the usual construction work is in progress, including the repositioning of a blast shield and the closure of Runway 09 Right/27 Left some nights for construction.

Once the flightplan has been examined, the crew then compare the co-ordinates for Track Victor as outlined in the flightplan with a separate print-out of the day's NAT tracks to ensure there is no discrepancy. As will soon become apparent, this is the first of many checks and balances designed to catch navigational errors before they cause problems.

As the Captain gathers up the paperwork, Don walks over to one of several computer terminals to get the latest weather reports. The computer print-out holds promising news. Good weather is forecast for both Toronto and London and there is nothing significant reported for the *en route* or alternate airports. The winds aloft forecast

*Right:*

**Weather chart depicting forecast upper wind velocities and temperatures at FL340. Wind direction is shown by the arrow and strength by the number of feathers on the tail. The chart indicates that the flight should enjoy strong tailwinds over the Atlantic.**

promises a strong tailwind for the duration of the flight that should help the crew pick up some lost time.

The two pilots are now ready to board so with paperwork in hand and bags in tow, they take the elevator back down to the departures level of the terminal and make their way to the gate. It's 2359Z, about 30min before the revised departure time, and much preparation remains to be done on board the aircraft. But before they can get to the aircraft, the crew first have to pass through airport security. Though hijackings seem to have fallen out of vogue with the world's terrorists, governments and airlines remain on guard against security threats, especially bombings like the ones believed to have downed an Air India flight over

```
NOTAMS
TORONTO INTL
  ..NDB X 385 U/S 9307011200 TIL 9307011700.
  ..ATTN AC873 CREWS...CP873 OPR YYZ AIRSPACE SAME TIME.
  ..ATTN AC800 CREWS: CANADIAN 800 OPR SAME TIME AS AC800. CTN ADVISED
  ..NEW WAT CHARTS FOR RWY 33 INTERSECTION TAKE-OFF
    SEE OPS TX CFWTL REGULAR YYZ UNTIL NEXT XMTL
  ..TRANSATLANTIC FLT CREWS - FOR OPTIMUM ALT AND ROUTE ON THE NAT -
    GANDER FSS REQUIRE A COAST OUT FIX ESTIMATE (CFE) - SEND TO YQX
    VIA HF FREQ P 5616 S 2899 TO INCLUDE A/C IDENT COAST OUT FIX/
    ESTIMATE/ AND MAX ACCEPTABLE FLT LEVEL AT OCEANIC BOUNDARY. SEND
    CFE 90 TO 120 MINUTES PRIOR TO COASTOUT. DO NOT SEND VIA YUL ATC
    OR ACARS.
  ..FLT 945 EX YYZ (WITH PUSH-BACK APRX 0615L) MUST NOT TAKE OFF
    PRIOR 0630L.
    PART     TWO CONT            0856/30 YYZ/LHR
;30JUN2300 FLQ 258


LONDON LHR
  ..REF DEP INFO 3 CHART DTD 21 JAN 93. DEP SEQUENCE NOTE 3. START
    UP CLEARANCE FREQ 121.7 CHNGD TO 121.97.
  ..HEATHROW DELIVERY - START-UP CLEARANCE FREQ CHNGD TO 121.97.
  ..RWY 09R/27L U/S DUE WIP BLOCK 85. 2130/0500 MON TO SAT NGTS TIL
    07100500.
  ..HIGH LEVEL HOLD ESTABLISHED AT MALBY INT. INBND TRACK 106 DEG
    MAG, TURNING LEFT AT 32 DME CPT AND TURNING INBND AT 50 DME CPT.
  ..RWY S 09R/27L IRVR U/S TIL APRX 07041700.
  ..NORTH SECTION OF ECHO CUL DE SAC BLAST SCREEN TO BE REPOSITIONED
    43 FT SOUTH OF PRESENT POSITION. ACFT MANOEUVRING TO STANDS E3
    AND E36 TO EXERCISE CAUTION.
  ..RWY 05/23 U/S U/S LDG AND T/O. ASSOCIATED LIGHTING AND TWY
    AFFECTED TIL 9310312359.
  ..DUE MAJOR TWY DEVELOPMENT OUTER TWY BLKS 38(O) 47(O) 63(O)
    62(O) AND 61(O) U/S. TWY RTE BTWN BLKS 78 AND 53 DIVERTED TO
    THE EAST OF THESE BLKS AND IS MARKED WITH DIVERTED YELLOW C/L
    GREEN REFLECTIVE C/L STUDS AND BLUE EDGE LGTS. CTN ADVSD
    AND FOLLOW MARKED DIVERTED C/L. TIL APRX 08121700.
```

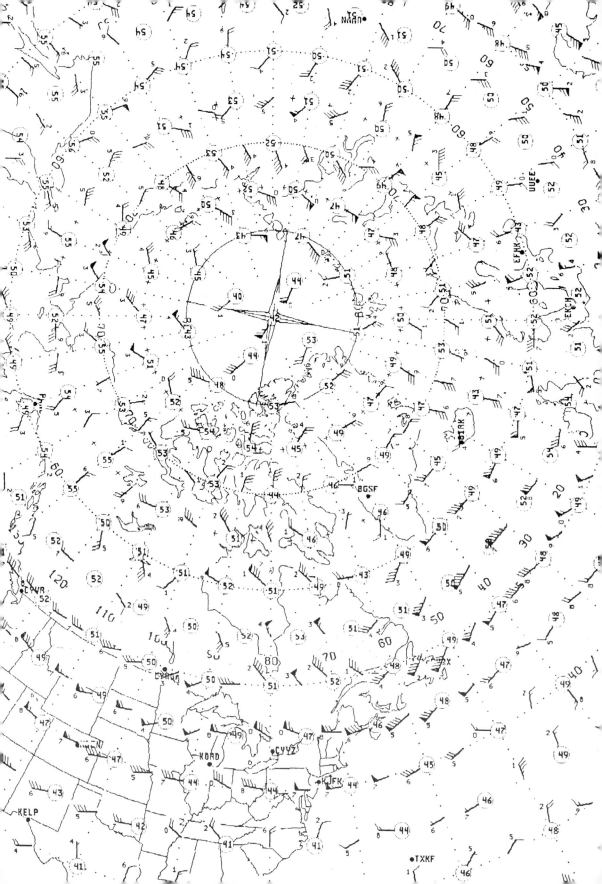

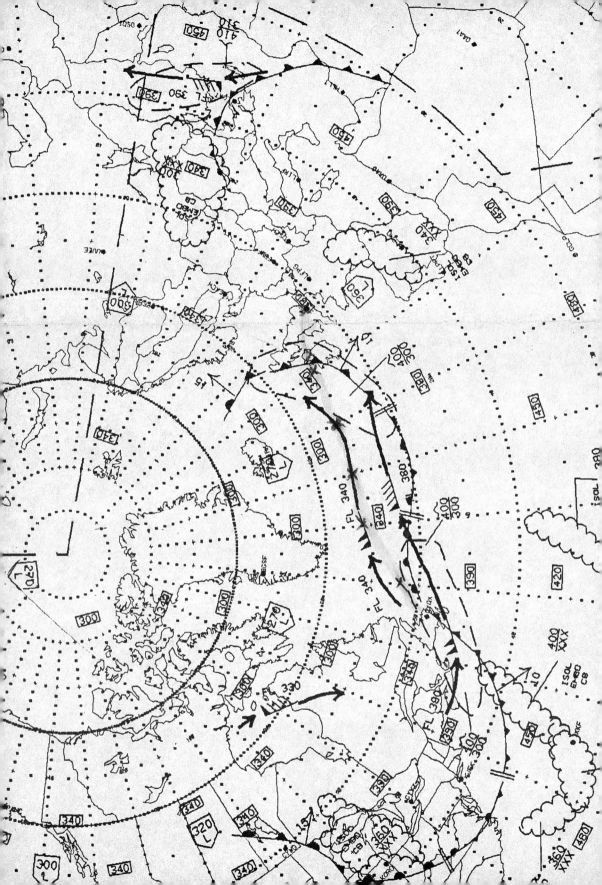

*Left:*
**The Significant Weather Chart for the North Atlantic.**

the North Atlantic and a Pan Am flight over Scotland. All passengers are required to pass through the security screening and have their hand luggage X-rayed. Most times, pilots are spared these rigorous checks and this is the case today as Bob and Don show security staff their bright green identification passes and are allowed through.

Once through security, it's a short walk to the international wing of the terminal and Gate 106, where the Boeing 747-400 allocated to Air Canada 856 is parked. Their aircraft today is C-GAGM, tail number 342. The aircraft has been in use for about a year and a half and in that time has logged 5,277 flying hours and 1,029 landings. Given that the jet has a design-life of 20 years or more in service, this aircraft is virtually brand-new. The large nose of the jet fills a window in the departure lounge and the ramp below is the scene of last-minute activity as the flight is prepared for departure.

Some of the passengers for the flight have begun to gather in the departures lounge and they try to pass the final few moments before their overseas journey commences; some grab a drink in a nearby restaurant or wander through the stores that dot the international wing. Others are content to sit and take in all the hustle and bustle. Business and First Class passengers are invited to await the boarding in a separate area that offers beverages and facilities, such as fax machines, for business travellers.

Don and Bob walk past the check-in counter and make their way along the docking pier to the aircraft. Traditionally, pilots perform one last inspection of their aircraft before departure to ensure that nothing glaring is amiss. Walking around the aircraft, the pilots look for oil leaks, open doors, damaged tyres and the like. Certainly with the sophistication of today's jets there's not much that a pilot can spot from the outside. One benefit of departing from Toronto though, is that the walk-around is done by the airline's maintenance staff, something that is appreciated by pilots on cold and snowy days.

Stepping through the large door, the cabin of the 747 appears immense. Row after row of seats appear to stretch for ever, divided by bulkheads, galleys and washrooms. In fact, the Wright Brothers' first flight at Kitty Hawk could have been performed within the length of the 150ft (45m) economy section of the 747-400. The 747-400 has the greatest passenger interior volume of any commercial airliner at 31,285cu ft (876cu m), the equivalent of more than three 1,500sq ft houses.

Economy seating is configured in a 3-4-3 arrangement that gives way to spacious 2-2 seating in the First Class compartment in the nose. The Business section is located on the upper deck with a single-aisle 2-2 arrangement. The 13 flight attendants, including the Flight Service Director, are already on board and are busy with their own preparations for the flight. The cabin crew arrived

**Towing the aircraft to the gate in preparation for the evening flight. . .**

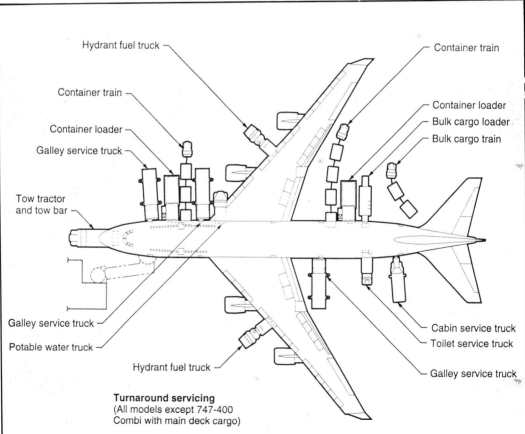

Hydrant fuel truck

Container train

Container train

Container loader

Galley service truck

Container loader
Bulk cargo loader
Bulk cargo train

Tow tractor
and tow bar

Galley service truck

Potable water truck

Cabin service truck
Toilet service truck

Hydrant fuel truck

Galley service truck

**Turnaround servicing**
(All models except 747-400
Combi with main deck cargo)

at the airport about 80min before departure and their first stop was a briefing held by the Flight Service Director, the in-charge flight attendant. The 20min briefing covers various safety aspects of the flight, such as actions required in the event of an evacuation or a sick passenger. The director also assigns working positions for the flight attendants and goes over the timing of the meals and movies during the flight. For the next seven hours, the aircraft will be home to nearly 300 people and a multitude of items are stored on board for their comfort: newspapers, magazines, headsets, pillows, blankets, children's activity books and, of course, airsickness bags. According to one 747 operator, no less than five and half tons of food supplies and more than 50,000 in-flight service items are needed on a typical international flight!

Several catering trucks are parked alongside the aircraft. The body of the trucks are raised on hydraulic jacks to the level of the cabin doors so the meal carts can be easily wheeled aboard. The meals were prepared by a catering firm at the airport less than six hours before departure and placed in cold storage until the flight; the dinner dishes have been pre-cooked and only require warming for seven to nine minutes in the galley ovens before serving. Initially, 220 meals are loaded and stowed in the galleys. Once a final passenger count is known in the minutes before departure, any extra meals that are required are loaded on board. Beverage carts stocked with enough for four drinks per passenger are also brought aboard. The carts actually have enough for the flight home to help reduce the turn-around time in London.

The Captain stops for a quick word of introduction with the Flight Service Director before joining Don upstairs on the flightdeck. A rest area containing two bunk beds is located at the rear of the flightdeck on the port side. The area is utilised only by crews flying very long-haul journeys and since it won't be needed today, it provides the perfect spot for the pilots to stow their bags. Don's first task is to turn on the auxiliary power unit (APU). This is a small jet engine located in the aircraft's tailcone that supplies bleed air for engine start and cabin air-conditioning and drives two electrical generators to supply power to the aircraft's electical system. The cabin of the aircraft is somewhat stuffy so Don checks that the APU bleed air valve is open and turns on the three air-conditioning packs and two recirculating fans to begin cooling the jet in preparation for the boarding of passengers.

At this point, each pilot begins his own series of detailed duties to check the condition of the flightdeck before take-off. Before settling into his seat, Don ensures that the overhead emergency hatch is latched shut, emergency equipment, like fire extinguishers and axe, oxygen and smoke masks and flashlights, are in place and that the document pouch, containing the aircraft certificates required on board, is sealed and in place on the back of the flightdeck door. He also does a quick check of the library of books and manuals needed on board. The books include the aircraft operating manual, the manual for the Flight Management System, minimum equipment lists (MEL) and chartbooks

**Preparing an aircraft for an overseas flight is a huge logistical task. Drink and meal carts are among the myriad of supplies needed for the flight ahead.**

for airports that could be used in the event of an emergency diversion. The Captain meanwhile has checked the electrics, ensured that the standby power is set to AUTO, examined the overhead circuit breaker board and reviewed the journey logbook and found that the aircraft has no outstanding snags or mechanical bugs.

He has also set the three inertial reference units that make up the IRS to NAV and inserted the latitude and longitude of the current aircraft position into the FMC to enable the IRS to align. Explaining the operation of the IRS would fill a textbook. Simply put, the IRS is a self-sufficient navigational system that uses ring laser gyros and sensitive accelerometers to detect and measure the slightest aircraft movement and thereby determine aircraft position. However, the system must have a starting reference point to calculate all other information so the aircraft's current position is entered into the IRS as part of the pre-flight tasks.

During the time it takes to align, each IRU determines the direction of local vertical and true north. The systems assume that local vertical is in the direction of the acceleration being sensed by the accelerometers (the earth's gravity) and by assuming that true north is along the axis of rotation being sensed by the laser gyros (the earth's rotation). Using the initial latitude and longitude of the aircraft on the gate, the IRS aligns itself and all further navigational calculations are based on this position.

**The Captain enters the waypoints into the FMC as they are read off the flight log by the First Officer.**

For the trip to London, the Captain has elected to be the non-flying pilot and will handle the radio calls and the navigation log. As the flying pilot, Don is responsible for the methodical pre-flight check of the cockpit instrumentation. The check begins at the overhead systems panel and continues across the auto-pilot controls on the glareshield, the standby instruments on the instrument panel, the EICAS displays and down the centre console with the speed brake, thrust levers, flap control and ending at the audio panel. The detailed procedure takes up several pages in the pilots' operating manual but includes opening fuel crossfeed valves, turning on the cockpit window heat (to prevent frosting and provide resiliency in the event of a bird strike) and testing the fire detection system.

The ATIS frequency of 133.1 MHz is selected on the right VHF so the pilots can listen to the Toronto Automated Terminal Information Service, a report of airport conditions that is updated regularly.

**Toronto ATIS:** 'This is Toronto International Airport Information Lima. Toronto weather at two three zero zero Zulu, four thousand scattered, one zero thousand scattered, three zero thousand scattered, visibility two five, temperature two zero, dewpoint one one, wind one six zero at four knots, altimeter three zero one zero. Departure runway is zero six right and three three. Voice advisory: simultaneous landings and departures are in effect on runway zero six left and runway three three. When requested to hold short of runway three three, landing distance available on runway zero six left is eight thousand three hundred and fifty feet. Inform Toronto ATC on initial contact that you have received information Lima.'

With individual duties complete, the crew come together to program the flightplan route into the FMC using the two CDUs located just in front of the thrust levers. The pilots can select information from the FMC through various pages such as navigation, holds and performance. In many cases, the system's database already contains standard routeings for flights routinely flown by the airline, like Toronto to Montreal. But because the tracks over the Atlantic change daily, the routeing to Heathrow must be entered manually.

Don reads off the waypoints one by one and watches carefully as the Captain punches them into the system. Once the routeing has been entered, the Captain then reads it back to the First Officer who verifies it against the flightplan. The rigorous procedure of checks and doublechecks guards against errors creeping into the system. As anyone familiar with computers knows 'garbage in, garbage out' and the FMC is no exception. For all its sophistication, the FMC is only as good as the information it gets from the pilots. It's more than capable of flying the aircraft in the wrong direction! The read-back by the Captain checks out and Don says 'Activate and Execute' and the flightplan is activated.

Next to be entered are the forecast winds aloft for each waypoint along the route. This, combined with the actual winds encountered *en route*, will enable the computer to calculate ETAs and estimate fuel burn during the flight. The equal fuel point is then entered into the FMC. Before this point, the aircraft will go to Goose Bay, located in Labrador, in case an *en route* diversion becomes necessary. After this point, the aircraft will proceed on to Shannon.

Don now starts into the take-off calculations, using the preliminary load figures contained in the flightplan. Once boarding is completed, the actual weight figures will be computed and sent to the crew via ACARS before departure for verification.

The estimated zero fuel weight of the aircraft, with passengers, cargo and baggage, is 239,300kg. The jet will be loaded with 80,200kg of fuel which includes 62,100kg for the actual flight; 9,400kg diversion fuel to fly to Glasgow, which has been picked as the landing alternate airport; 1,400kg

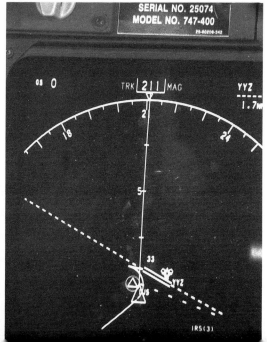

The ND set at 10nm range showing the aircraft, displayed as the white triangle, at the gate and the departure runway. Above the ND are the controls for switching displays in case a CRT fails.

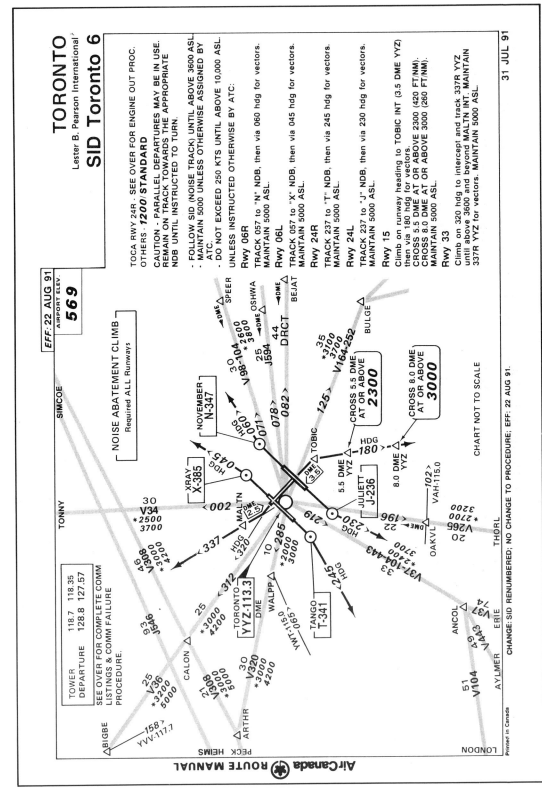

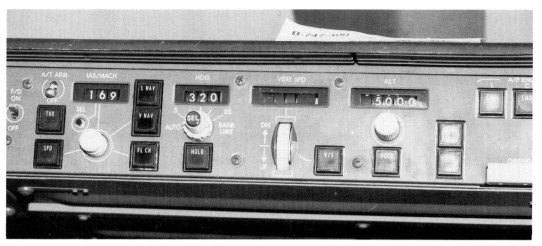

*Left:*
**Chart showing the Toronto 6 Standard Instrument Departure routeings.** *Air Canada*

*Above:*
**The auto-pilot and flight director system is controlled by the pilots through a selector panel on the glareshield above the instrument panel. The three knobs set airspeed, heading and altitude while other controls select auto-flight and flight director modes. Seen here, the controls are set for a Standard Instrument Departure from Runway 33.**

for taxying at Toronto; and 3,100kg to cover any contingencies, such as headwinds. With the fuel load added in, the estimated take-off weight will be 318,000kg, well under the maximum of 347,900kg. In many cases, full thrust is not required for take-off and a lower thrust setting is used to extend engine life. Don pulls a manual from his briefcase and opens it to a weight and temperature take-off performance chart for the expected departure runway. Extrapolating from the chart, Don finds that at the planned take-off weight (plus 15,000kg added as a safety cushion), something less than maximum power will be sufficient for take-off. From the chart, he extracts an assumed temperature of 40° Celsius which is entered into the FMC. The system then calculates the full power setting required for take-off at that temperature which in turn results in a graduated take-off setting at today's temperature: an Engine Pressure Ratio (EPR) of 1.40 which is automatically displayed on the EPR tapes on the EICAS. EPR measures the ratio of the LPT (Low Pressure Turbine) exhaust pressure to the engine inlet pressure and is the prime reference in setting power.

Don then calls up the Take-Off reference page on the FMC and enters the take-off flap setting of 10° and 3,000ft, the altitude at which the flight director, or auto-pilot if it is engaged, will command a lower pitch during the climb so the air-

craft can accelerate for flap retraction. The FMC calculates the flap retraction speeds and automatically displays them on the airspeed tape. Next, the engine out acceleration altitude of 600ft is entered into the FMC. If the jet loses an engine during take-off, the flight director will command a lower pitch attitude to gain speed and clean up the aircraft sooner than normal. With its tremendous thrust, the 747-400 is easily able to climb after losing an engine. Finally, 1,500ft is entered as the altitude at which the auto-throttles will reduce engine thrust to climb power.

With the aircraft's zero fuel weight now inputted, the FMC adds this to the fuel load, which it automatically senses and calculates the important V-speeds for take-off: V1, the decision speed, is 146kt; VR, or rotation speed, is 157kt; and V2, the safe climb-out speed if an engine is lost after V1, is 169kt. An emergency during take-off is one of the few that demands split second decisions and actions by the pilots. Take-offs are aborted for only the most serious of emergencies like an engine fire, loss of power in an engine, or an obstacle on the runway. Thanks to instincts and skills honed in training, the crew will react instinctively when a take-off must be aborted. V1 is known as the go/no go speed. If an emergency occurs before that speed, the Captain will call 'reject'. Obviously an abort close to V1 is a serious matter in itself as maximum braking is applied to stop the aircraft on the remaining stretch of runway. If the emergency happens after V1, the crew will take-off in a normal fashion, get the gear up and ensure the jet is safely in a climb before dealing with the crisis. The first priority is to fly the aircraft. More than one pilot has allowed an emergency to distract them from the task of flying the aircraft, sometimes with disastrous results. After confirmation by the pilots, the V-speeds are automatically 'bugged' on the airspeed tape.

By now, the IRUs have aligned and the PFDs

and NDs come alive as they begin receiving navigational and flight data from the IRS. Bob and Don check that 211° is shown as the heading on their respective NDs and the compass rose at the bottom of the PFDs, cross-check altitudes and altimeter settings to catch any discrepancies, ensure that brake pressure, shown on an analogue gauge below the Captain's ND, is in the green and check for any warning flags.

With a well-oiled routine born from experience, the pilots rehearse the actions they will take in the unlikely event of an emergency during take-off. If an incident happens prior to V1, the Captain states that he will close the thrust levers and will **confirm maximum braking is taking effect.**

**First Officer:** 'I'll push forward on the control column, check that the spoiler lever is up, call spoilers up or no spoilers. I will call operating or no reverse for the particular engine. I will call the airspeeds and I'll stand by to advise ATC.'

**Captain:** 'Operating symmetrical engines, I'll bring the aircraft to a halt, set the parking brakes and perform any abnormalities. If it's catastrophic, I'll call severe aircraft damage and I'll tell the passengers what side to evacuate on.'

**First officer:** 'If you call severe aircraft damage, I'll set the spoilers down, the fuel control switches to cut-off, manually open the outflow valves. The engine and APU fire switches I'll pull and discharge the bottles.'

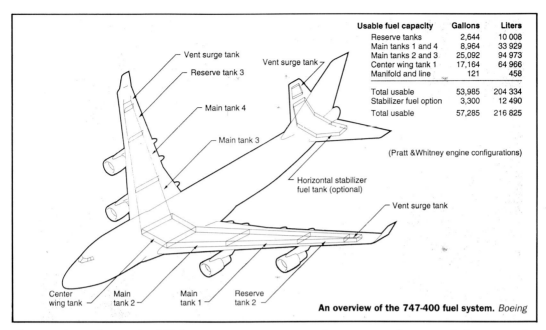

| Usable fuel capacity | Gallons | Liters |
|---|---|---|
| Reserve tanks | 2,644 | 10 008 |
| Main tanks 1 and 4 | 8,964 | 33 929 |
| Main tanks 2 and 3 | 25,092 | 94 973 |
| Center wing tank 1 | 17,164 | 64 966 |
| Manifold and line | 121 | 458 |
| Total usable | 53,985 | 204 334 |
| Stabilizer fuel option | 3,300 | 12 490 |
| Total usable | 57,285 | 216 825 |

(Pratt &Whitney engine configurations)

**An overview of the 747-400 fuel system.** *Boeing*

The crew then rehearse the drill for an emergency after V1.

**Captain:** 'Okay, going along the runway after V1, I'll say fire number four.'
**First Officer:** 'I'll continue the take-off, normal rotation and lift-off.'
**Captain:** 'Positive rate.'
**First Officer:** 'I'll call for power and the gear up.'
**Captain:** 'Power's up, gear's up.'
**First Officer:** 'When established in the climb at a minimum of V2, I will call for the engine fire drill.'
**Captain:** 'I will recheck that the gear is up, power is up. Number four throttle. . .'
**First Officer:** 'I'll confirm the engine. Close.'
**Captain:** 'Number four fuel control. . .'
**First Officer:** 'Cut off.'
**Captain:** 'Number four fire switch. . . '
**First Officer:** 'Pull.'
**Captain:** 'I'll pull the handle. If the light stays on the EICAS, I'll discharge the first shot, check the time, thirty seconds and if the light is still on, I'll discharge the second.'
**First Officer:** 'I'll continue the climb at V2 to TOCA (Terrain Obstacle Clearance Altitude), accel-

erate, clean up on the normal flap retraction schedule. Somewhere above fifteen hundred feet, I'll call for checklist, engine fire.'

The emergency drill is done and Don calls clearance delivery on 121.3.

**First Officer R/T:** 'Toronto Clearance Delivery, it's Air Canada eight five six heavy at Gate one-oh-six with Lima.'
**Clearance Delivery:** 'Air Canada eight five six heavy, cleared to London Heathrow via Toronto six departure, zero seven eight radial, J-five nine four to Massena, flight planned route, take-off thirty-three. Squawk two two six six.'

The First Officer reads back the clearance and tunes 2266 in the transponder.

The multitude of departure tasks are now nearly done and the pilots are ready to go. The boarding call has gone out in the departures lounge and the passengers have collected their personal belongings, reached for their tickets and headed to the gate with an air of anticipation. Boarding is still in progress and Don takes advantage of the time to do the departure briefing. The take-off will be to the northwest from Runway 33 following the Standard Instrument Departure.

The SID for Runway 33 is designed for noise abatement and steers aircraft clear of several residential neighbourhoods north of the airport. It calls for a left turn after take-off to a heading of 320° to intercept the 337° radial from the Toronto VOR, a radio beacon located in the middle of the airfield. After intercepting the 337° radial, the jet

*Left:*
**The large rear door enables bulky pallets of cargo to be loaded into the main deck cargo area behind the passenger cabin. The cargo area lacks the aesthetic sidewall and overhead panelling, providing a glimpse at the tubing, wiring and insulation normally hidden from view.**

will turn right to track the radial to 5,000ft until further clearance from ATC. Reaching to the auto-flight controls on the glareshield, Don dials up 320 in the heading window, 169 on the airspeed and 5,000 on the altitude. It's now 0025Z and with the flight's departure time just five minutes away, Don calls the airline's nerve centre, called the Station Operations Centre (STOC) for an update.

**First Officer R/T:** 'Hello STOC, it's eight five six. Any idea what time we're going to be out of here?'
**STOC R/T:** 'Yes, I was just about to call you. It looks like (eight) forty-five (local time).'

The crew find that they have to wait a bit longer before departure but the extra few minutes aren't all bad. Bob reaches for the Captain's headset only to find that it has gone missing. He calls maintenance on the radio and asks for a new one. It's not long before a maintenance employee arrives with a replacement headset. As the clock ticks down to take-off, the boggling multitude of tasks that go into a transatlantic flight are completed one by one. Fuelling is now finished and the refueller enters the flightdeck to present the fuel sheet to the Captain with the final figures. The jet is quickly fuelled by using the refuelling stations located on the lower leading edge between the two engines on each wing. A fuel truck parked under the left wing has one hose connected to an underground hydrant which is piped into the airport fuel farm where large tanks store thousands of litres of jet fuel. Another hose is hooked into the underwing fuelling port and the fuel is pumped by the truck to this single refuelling point and distributed throughout the aircraft's fuel tanks. In this case, the jet has been loaded with 80,200kg of Jet A fuel, a quarter of the aircraft's total take-off weight: 4,000kg in the two reserve tanks, 13,600kg in the two outboard main tanks and 22,450kg in the two inboard mains. The interior of the jet's wings is coated with a sealant to make it fuel-tight, forming giant fuel tanks. The tanks are inter-connected by a series of valves and the fuel is piped to the engines by powerful pumps. On the route to London, the wing fuel tanks hold the required fuel load and it's rare to use the centre and stabiliser tanks. In fact, today's flight will hardly stretch the aircraft's legs at all — the design range of the 747-400 Combi is 6,590nm, double the length of a Toronto-Heathrow flight.

A ground crew employee presents the crew with the hazardous material manifest showing that the flight is carrying two 20 litre containers of resin. The document has been signed off by the groundcrew that the material is packaged properly and safely stowed.

The Flight Service Director pops in and reports that there are 281 passengers and two infants on board. Bob takes a few moments on the PA to welcome the passengers on board, apologise for the delay and explain the flight's route.

The door synoptic on the lower EICAS CRT shows that the upper deck and cargo doors on the left side and the aft cargo and bulk cargo doors on the right are still open. As the groundcrew finish their work, the door lights go out one by one until only the upper deck passenger door remains open.

**Passing the final few minutes before pushback.**

# Departure

A muffled clunk is heard from below on the port side as the last cabin door is swung shut. Moments later, the lead station attendant, the groundcrew member overseeing the departure, is calling on the aircraft intercom. Air Canada 856 is ready to go. The last of the holds are now closed, the chocks have been pulled clear of the wheels and the docking bridge has been retracted. A tow-bar and heavy squat tractor are connected to the nosewheel ready to push the big jet back from the terminal. The Captain acknowledges the ground-crew and calls 'Before Start check'.

**First Officer:** 'Parking brake.'
**Captain:** 'Set.'
**First Officer:** 'External power.'
**Captain:** 'Disconnected.'
**First Officer:** 'Hydraulics.'
**Captain:** 'Set.' (Three pumps are set to auto and the fourth is set to auxiliary to power the brakes during pushback)
**First Officer:** 'Fuel quantity and pumps.'
**Captain:** 'Checked on.'
**First Officer:** 'Packs.' (Referring to the air-conditioning packs).
**Captain:** 'Set.'
**First Officer:** 'Beacon.'
**Captain:** 'Both.' (Two red strobe lights on the top and bottom of the fuselage begin flashing.)
**First Officer:** 'Status.'
**Captain:** 'Checked.' (The Captain checks the lower EICAS for any messages).
**First Officer:** 'Doors.'
**Captain:** 'Closed.'
**First Officer:** 'Seatbelts.'
**Captain:** 'Automatic.'
**First Officer:** 'Before Start check complete.'

Don calls the Apron controller, who is responsible for movement on the tarmac around the terminal, for clearance to push back and start-up.

**First Officer R/T:** 'Air Canada eight five six, gate one-oh-six push.'
**Apron:** 'Air Canada eight five six push at your discretion, call for taxi.'

Don acknowledges the clearance and the Captain passes it on to the ground staff. Out of sight below the nose, a loud growl is heard as the tractor pushes the aircraft smoothly move away from the terminal. It's 0058Z.

After pushback, the aircraft must be towed a short distance away from the other gates before engine start is permitted to avoid damaging nearby aircraft with the jet blast. Linked to the flightdeck by an intercom hook-up on the nosegear, the lead station attendant walks with the aircraft, joined by other ground staff. The ramp around the terminal is a crowded place with catering trucks, baggage carts, fuel trucks and a multitude of other vehicles darting to and fro. The pilots have no way of seeing behind the aircraft during pushback and rely on the ground crew to be their eyes to ensure the big jet doesn't run into anything. Even a small dent in the fuselage can cost thousands of dollars to repair not to mention the inconvenience of the resulting delays for passengers. Once the aircraft is clear, the station attendant is calling again on the intercom.

**Ground engineer:** 'Okay Captain, you're clear to start engines.'

The Captain replies on the intercom 'Starting one, two, three, four' and then turns to Don and commands 'Start One'.

On cue, the First Officer reaches to the overhead panel and pulls open the start valve for engine number one. Bleed air from the APU is fed into the engine to spin the N2 compressor to the speed necessary for light-up. Primary engine information is displayed on the upper EICAS display and secondary engine information, such as N2 and oil temperature and pressure, is shown on the lower EICAS display during the engine start. N2 begins to rise slowly. Both pilots carefully monitor the engine indications, alert for any sign of a bad start.

At about 25% N2 (the exact value is determined by the FMC and shown as a magenta line on the N2 display) and oil pressure confirmed rising, Bob moves the engine's fuel cock, located immediately behind the thrust lever, to the open position, introducing fuel into the engine and enabling ignition. He calls 'Fuel on run' and Don starts his stop-watch. Normally, only one of the engine's two ignition systems is used for start. But if ignition is not obtained after 20sec, the ignition system on the overhead panel will be selected to

# TORONTO, Ont
Lester B. Pearson International
## GROUND MOVEMENT

### Taxi restrictions

**①** TWY C - DO NOT ENTER from TWY D. ... ONE WAY INBOUND ONLY.... DO NOT CROSS AMBER LIGHTS ⊕ installed in pavement at junction of TWY D EXCEPT when exiting runway towards terminal.

**②** TWY F & X - Normally ONE WAY INBND ONLY. DO NOT proceed beyond AMBER LIGHTS ⊕ installed in pavement on HOLD LINES without CLEARANCE except when exiting runway towards terminal.

⊕NOTE: AMBER LGTS visible only when taxiing outbnd from terminal towards runways.

- TWY U, M & W uncontrolled.

**③** CAUTION advised when TURNING RIGHT from rwy 33. NOT AUTHORIZED when rwy or twy surface contaminated and strong NW winds exist.

| | | |
|---|---|---|
| ATIS | 113.3 | 114.8 |
| ⊕CLNC DEL (PT) | 120.82 | 133.1 |
| GRND | 121.3 | |
| | 121.9 | 121.65 |
| APRON | 122.07 | |
| TOWER | 118.7 | 118.35 |

⊕0700-2300L.

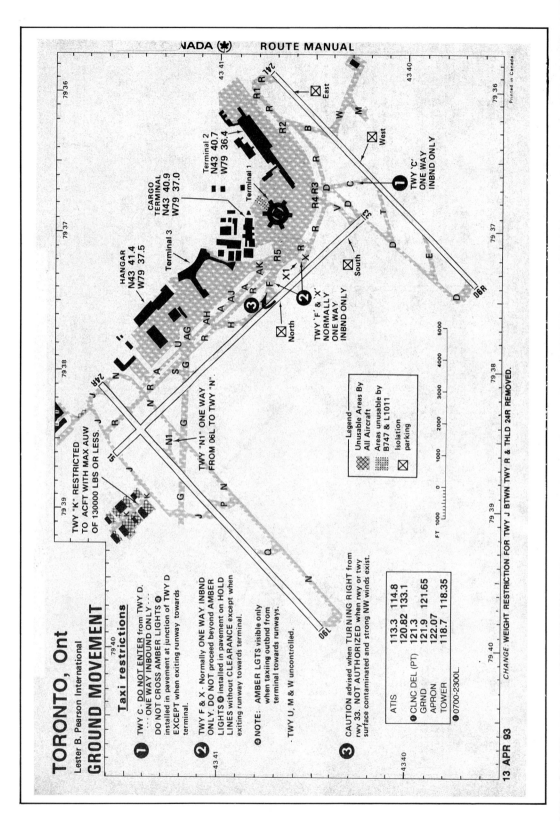

TWY "K" RESTRICTED TO ACFT WITH MAX AUW OF 130000 LBS OR LESS.

TWY "N1" ONE WAY FROM 06L TO TWY "N".

TWY 'F' & 'X' NORMALLY ONE WAY INBND ONLY

TWY 'C' ONE WAY INBND ONLY

East

West

South

North

HANGAR N43 41.4 W79 37.5

Terminal 3

Terminal 2 N43 40.7 W79 36.4

Terminal 1

CARGO TERMINAL N43 40.9 W79 37.0

**Legend**

⊠ Unusable Areas By All Aircraft

Areas unusable by B747 & L1011

⊠ Isolation parking

FT 1000   0   1000   2000   3000   4000   5000

43 41   79 40   79 39   79 38   79 37   79 36

43 40

**13 APR 93**   CHANGE: WEIGHT RESTRICTION FOR TWY J BTWN TWY R & THLD 24R REMOVED.

Printed in Canada

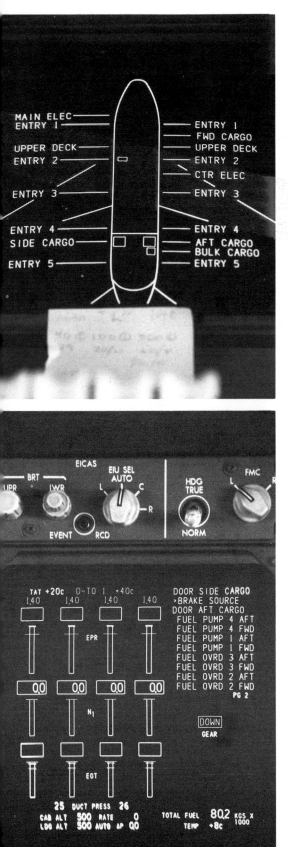

'BOTH' which usually results in a start. In less than 10sec the EGT and N1 rise rapidly, confirming that the engine has started. The crew keep a close eye on the EGT to guard against a 'hot start' when engine temperatures threaten to exceed the maximum limit of 550° Celsius. In that case, the fuel is shut off and the engine is turned for 30sec to clear out the excess fuel and cool the core before a restart is attempted. At about 50% N2, the engine is self-sustaining and the spring-loaded start valve snaps back into place. The start is a normal one and the number one engine settles into idle at 1.01 EPR, 23.8% N1, EGT of 316 Celsius, N2 of 64% and a fuel flow of 600kg/hr.

Air Canada's 747-400s are powered by four Pratt and Whitney 4056-series powerplant, a two-spool, axial-flow turbofan which each produce 56,000lb of thrust. Thrust is provided by two separate airflow paths, primary and secondary. The primary airflow path is drawn into the engine core where it is compressed by the N1 and N2 compressors and then mixed with burning fuel. The hot exhaust gases expand rapidly and race out the rear, passing through a series of turbines which drive the compressors. The primary flow accounts for 20% of the thrust. The secondary, or fan airflow, passes through the N1 compressor which is the large ring of blades visible at the front of the engine. Driven by a turbine in the engine, the N1 compressor acts very much like a propeller and produces 80% of the engine thrust. The engine has a 5:1 bypass ratio — for every part of air that enters the engine core, five parts pass through the N1 compressor and around the core.

The tow is complete and the station attendant breaks into the start routine.

**Ground:** 'Ground to flightdeck, confirm brakes set.'

**The upper EICAS display shown before engine start. The top row of displays show EPR for each engine with N1 below and EGT on the bottom. The 1.40 shown above each EPR tape is the selected take-off EPR. On the right is the message list, showing numerous warnings that will extinguish as the engines are started. The gear down indication and the total fuel load are also visible.**

The Captain presses the top of the rudder pedals and at the same time pulls up the parking brake lever located just behind the speed-brake on the centre console. He confirms that the brakes are set and the ground staff replies that the pins have been removed. This last comment refers to the nosegear bypass steering pins that are inserted by the ground crew into the nosegear to bypass the cockpit steering and allow the nosewheel to turn freely during pushback and tow.

The remaining three engines are started in normal fashion. Outside, the noise from the turbines is ear-piercing but on the flightdeck only a muted growl is heard as the Captain calls for 'After Start Checks'.

**First Officer:** 'APU.'
**Captain:** 'Off.'
**First Officer:** 'Demand Pumps.'
**Captain:** 'Auto.' (The fourth hydraulic pump is now set to auto.)
**First Officer:** 'Nacelle anti-ice.'
**Captain:** 'Off.'

*Right:*
**Before Start check. Running through the checks, the air-conditioning packs are set to normal.**

*Below:*
**Pushback.**

*Above:*
**The main gear.**

*Below:*
**The crew await the okay to start engines as the jumbo is towed clear of the gate.**

'Start Four.' The First Officer pulls open the start valve for the outboard starboard engine to begin the start sequence while the Captain monitors engine indications on the upper and lower EICAS displays.

First Officer: 'Aft cargo heat.'
Captain: 'On.'
First Officer: 'Packs.'
Captain: 'Normal.'
First Officer: 'Recall.'
Captain: 'Checked.' (The recall button on the glareshield is pressed to recall any outstanding EICAS messages that may have previously been cancelled by the crew.)
First Officer: 'Flaps.'
Captain: 'Ten flaps selected.'

Ten degrees of flap are used for most take-offs but 20° can be used to shorten the take-off roll if runway distance is a factor. With take-off flaps selected the fuel system automatically reconfigures. Crossfeed valves two and three automatically close, providing a tank to engine feed for take-off.

The lead station attendant wishes the crew a good flight before disconnecting and walking clear of the aircraft with the pushback tractor and other ground staff. Visible on the right side of the

Air Canada 856 taxies to the runway. Ten degrees of flap has been selected and the trailing and leading edge flaps deploy to the setting.

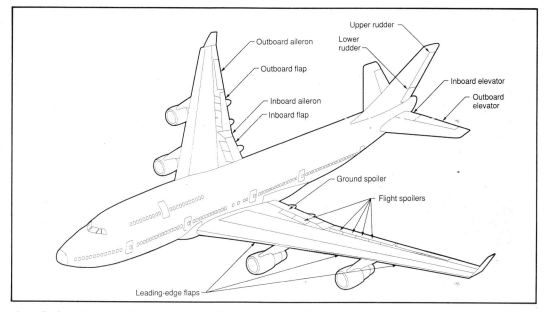

Outboard aileron
Outboard flap
Inboard aileron
Inboard flap
Upper rudder
Lower rudder
Inboard elevator
Outboard elevator
Ground spoiler
Flight spoilers
Leading-edge flaps

aircraft, he gives one last wave to indicate the way is clear.

The checks are complete and Don calls apron for taxi clearance. The First Officer handles the radio calls on the ground, leaving the Captain free to concentrate on taxying the jet.

**First Officer R/T:** 'Air Canada eight five six heavy, taxi.'
**Apron:** 'Air Canada eight five six, runway three-three via the apron, hold short of Romeo four.'

Bob releases the parking brake and each pilot makes a quick check out the side windows to ensure all is clear. The Captain eases forward on the throttles and quickly pulls them back — a touch of power is enough to get the jet rolling and the big turbofans provide plenty of residual thrust even at idle setting to keep it moving. Pilots try to avoid using large bursts of power during taxi which could easily injure crew members or damage equipment in the tight confines of the ramp area. Even at idle, the blast from the jet exhaust is felt 600ft behind the aircraft. Bob uses a steering tiller, located near his left knee on the cockpit sidewall, to steer the jet along the yellow line on the tarmac. The aircraft is supported by the nosegear with two wheels and four main gears: two body gears and two wing gears, each composed of a four-wheel truck. The tiller can turn the nosegear 70° either side of centre. The nose-wheel steering is assisted by body gear steering which automatically activates when the nosegear is turned more than 20° and the speed is below 15kt. The body gears turn opposite to the nosegear to assist the turn and avoid tyre scrubbing.

**The flight controls.** *Boeing*

Taxying a 747 is a bit like driving a tractor trailer, only this 'trailer' has a wingspan of 211ft (213ft when fully fuelled since the wingtips droop slightly from the weight of fuel in the wings.) The Captain must be careful in the turns to ensure the main bogies, located 84ft behind the nosewheel, don't drag in the grass. Perched some three storeys above the tarmac, it's easy to misjudge speed so to avoid taxying too fast, a ground speed read out is shown on the ND.

During the taxi, the pilots run through the Before Take-off checks, checking the heading indications; take-off data, like V-speeds is set; stabiliser trim is set at six units and rudder and aileron trim is checked set at neutral; and flaps are checked 10° selected and indicated on the upper EICAS display. The rudder, spoilers, ailerons and elevators are each moved to ensure full deflection and return to neutral position.

The auto-brake selector on the centre console is checked set to RTO (Rejected Take-off). The aircraft is equipped with auto-brakes which automatically provide smooth braking after landing. For normal landings, the selector is usually set to 1 or 2 to supply moderate braking during roll-out. This saves on brake wear and minimises discomfort for passengers. However, in the event of an aborted take-off, the priority is to slow the aircraft down. When RTO is selected, the auto-brakes will apply maximum braking pressure if the thrust levers are cut to idle and the speed is over 85kt during the take-off roll. As well, when reverse thrust is selected during an aborted take-off, the spoilers will automatically extend to spoil lift over the wings and place the aircraft's weight firmly on the wheels for improved braking.

The ND is checked set on MAP and range set at 10nm and VNAV is armed. Through the flight director bars on the PFD, VNAV will guide the pilots along the proper climb profile after take-off. At this point, the auto-throttle is also armed. The auto-throttle is left unarmed during the taxi to prevent its inadvertent selection which would cause the engines to spool up to take-off thrust on the ramp — definitely not a desirable situation.

Don tucks away the checklist and calls 'lights and strobes to go'. The landing and strobe lights are normally left off until the aircraft is on the runway. In the cabin, the flight attendants are tending to the passengers, helping them settle in and ensuring they are buckled up for take-off. The mandatory safety briefing for passengers is done by a recorded video shown on the video screens throughout the cabin with flight attendants pointing out the location of the nearest exits. The cabin doors have now been armed by the flight attendants and, if they are opened now, an emergency slide will automatically deploy and inflate to assist the emergency evacuation.

During the taxi, the final load figures are received via ACARS and are cross-checked with the estimates contained in the flightplan. With this information Don is able to confirm the aircraft's centre of gravity and trim setting required

**Taxying at Pearson.**

for take-off. The loading of the aircraft is done to ensure that the centre of gravity remains within prescribed limits. The aircraft could be dangerously nose or tail heavy and even uncontrollable if the centre of gravity was outside those limits. From the figures, Don determines that the centre of gravity is at 27% MAC (Mean Aerodynamic Chord). This is entered into the FMC which shows that a stabiliser trim setting of six units is required for take-off. This setting is checked set.

The jet rumbles along the ramp, methodically bumping on the cracks in the pavement as it passes the length of Terminal 2 and the fleet of Air Canada DC-9s, Airbus A320s and Boeing 767s which are parked at the gates. Terminal 2 is the hub of Air Canada's domestic and international network. Terminal 1, the airport's original terminal, also comes into view on the right side. Built in the 1960s, the terminal won accolades from designers for its circular design but was soon overtaken with the advent of the jets and their larger passenger loads. Just north of Terminal 1 is Terminal 3, the newest terminal which welcomed its first passengers in 1991. It was the first international terminal in Canada to be financed, built and operated by the private sector rather than government, following a trend that is being seen at airports around the world.

Pearson has two parallel runways aligned southwest/northeast and a third runway running roughly north-south. During peak periods, Pearson is effectively divided into two airports for the purpose of air traffic control. Aircraft departing for destinations to the east and south are assigned

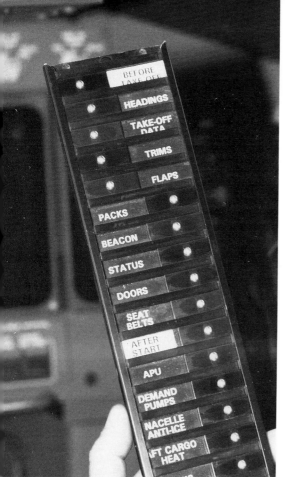

to the south parallel runway and aircraft bound for airports to the north and west are directed to the north parallel. Arriving aircraft are routed in the same fashion. The procedures split the air traffic in half between the two runways and greatly simplify air traffic control by eliminating the need to criss-cross traffic flows in the sky. Separate ground, tower, departure and arrival controllers are dedicated to the south and north operation.

By this time of night though, the pace has slackened off and the controllers are dispatching most flights from Runway 33. Nearing the taxiway, the apron controller calls and asks the flight to call the ground controller, who is located in the control tower on the west side of the airport. The frequency has already been dialled up on standby and is switched over to the active frequency.

**First Officer R/T:** 'Toronto Ground, it's Air Canada eight five six, short of Romeo three.'
**Toronto Ground:** 'Air Canada eight five six taxi Romeo three and Delta to thirty-three, altimeter three zero zero one.'

The jet snakes around a tight turn and on to Delta taxiway. The Captain slows the jet to a stop by pressing on the top of the rudder pedals which are connected to the brakes. Ground calls again and advises the flight to tune Toronto tower on 118.7. The white runway lights and the blue taxiway lights glitter in the twilight. An L-1011 TriStar belonging to Air Transat, a Canadian charter airline, can be seen in the distance as it turns final for Runway 06 Right. With a roar, an Air Canada DC-9 departs Runway 33 and a Canadian Airlines International Boeing 737 waiting on a parallel taxiway is cleared on to the runway.

On the PA, Don advises the flight attendants to take positions for take-off. The Canadian 737 begins its take-off roll and Toronto tower calls.

**Toronto Tower:** 'Air Canada eight five six heavy, position three-three, departure frequency will be one twenty-eight eight.'

Don reads back the clearance and switches on the landing and strobe lights on the overhead panel.

**With one hand on the tiller and the other on the throttles, the Captain guides the jet into position at the threshold.**

45

The Captain eases the throttles forward and the big jet lumbers on to the threshold of the runway. The compass rose across the top of the ND slowly turns to the runway heading of 327° as the jet swings to the right and lines up with the centre-line markings. The 'heavy' designation used as part of the callsign applies to all aircraft that are certified for a maximum take-off weight of 300,000lb or more. It is meant to alert controllers and other pilots that the flight is a large aircraft that will produce potentially dangerous wake turbulence. Just like a boat creates a wake in the water, aircraft leave an unseen trail of disturbed air and wingtip vortices in their wake as well. The larger the aircraft, the stronger the turbulence to the point that it could upset other smaller aircraft flying behind. For this reason, controllers allow extra separation between heavy aircraft and lighter aircraft, up to six miles in the case of a light twin-engine Cessna following a DC-10 or 747. Controllers will also delay departures behind a heavy jet to allow time for the air to settle.

Ahead, the 737 can be climbing into the dusk sky, banking to the left as it follows the SID. After just a short pause, the tower is again on the radio.

**Toronto Tower:** 'Air Canada eight five six heavy, departure frequency one twenty-eight eight in the air, cleared take-off three three.'

The brakes are released and Don throttles up to about 1.10 EPR and pauses momentarily to allow the engines to stabilise. If any of the so-called 'killer' items, like trim or flaps, were not properly set for take-off, a horn would sound at this point to alert the crew.

All is normal and Don presses the take-off/go-around (TO/GA) buttons on the front of the thrust levers. The auto-throttles take over and move the levers smoothly forward to the take-off power setting of 1.40 EPR. Activation of the TO/GA buttons also causes the FMC to update the aircraft's position. The gate co-ordinates entered during the pre-flight to align the IRS can sometimes cover a wide area. The FMC knows the exact co-ordinates of the runway threshold and using this more precise information, it updates the IRS. Like magic, the runway depicted on the ND shifts slightly and aligns exactly under the white triangle, which marks the aircraft's position.

A muffled roar is heard on the flightdeck as the four Pratt & Whitney engines spool up to take-off thrust and the aircraft begins its roll. The acceleration is brisk and the massive thrust presses the crew into their seats. Don is looking outside the cockpit, keeping the jet straight on the runway with gentle movements of the rudder pedals which are connected to the nosewheel. He glances at the airspeed tape, watching for the bugged airspeeds as the speed builds rapidly. The Captain divides his attention between the view outside, the airspeed tape and the EICAS display, checking that all is normal. After the engines are set at take-off power, the Captain puts his hand on the throttles, ready to abort if an emergency occurs.

Eighty knots passes and the bugged speeds appear at the top of the airspeed tape. A speed trend arrow on the tape confirms the brisk acceleration. At V1, the Captain takes his hand off the throttles: the aircraft is now committed to take-off and any emergency at this point will be handled in the air. VR — rotate. Don pulls smoothly back on the control column at about three degrees per second, rotating the aircraft to 15° pitch-up for take-off — not too fast or the tail could scrape the runway and not too slow or the take-off roll would be lengthened. The nosegear lifts off the runway followed by the main bogies and the jet climbs into the evening sky. It's 0112Z and Air Canada 856 is airborne after a take-off roll of 52sec and roughly 8,400ft. At 50ft off the ground, the Captain confirms that the aircraft is climbing.

**Captain:** 'Positive rate.'
**First Officer:** 'Gear up.'

The Captain reaches over and selects the gear handle to the UP position. Gear doors swing open on the jet's belly and nose. The four main bogies and the nose gear are retracted out of sight and the doors swing shut again. The green GEAR symbol on the upper EICAS display turns barber pole white, then white before disappearing, confirming that the gear is safely stowed. The noise level on the flightdeck drops noticeably as the gear is tucked away and the aircraft cleaned up.

Don is now flying on instruments and guides the aircraft symbol on the PFD just under the flight director bars which are commanding a climb at V2 + 10kt. HDG, or heading, is selected on the auto-flight control panel and the flight director commands a gentle left turn to 320° to fly the SID. Through 1,500 asl, the throttles move back slightly as the auto-throttle reduces thrust to climb power. The speed is 184kt and building as Don turns right to pick up the 337° radial from the Toronto VOR.

The Captain checks in with the departure controller.

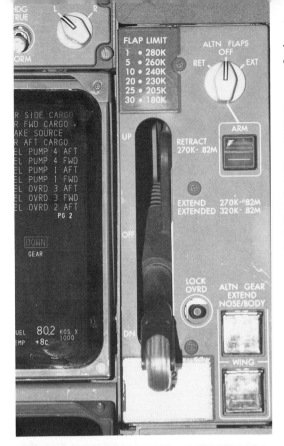

The gear handle is located to the right of the upper EICAS display. Note the alternate controls for flaps and gear.

**Toronto departure:** 'Air Canada eight five six heavy, departure radar identified, you're cleared to seven thousand.'

The aircraft is now under the control of the departure controller located in the Toronto Area Control Centre at Pearson who sits in a large windowless room unable to see outside. Instead, he relies on radar to be his 'eyes'. Sitting in front of a radar screen, the controller keeps careful watch over the green triangles on the screen, each one depicting the position of a different aircraft.

The departure controller is responsible for his own parcel of airspace and, as Air Canada 856 clears flights which are inbound to Toronto, he is able to let the jet climb progressively higher.

The new altitude is dialled up on the altitude window of the auto-flight control panel and selected. Through 3,000ft — the altitude programmed during pre-flight — the pitch bar on the flight director drops from about 15° to just under 10° so the aircraft can accelerate for flap retraction. Approaching 200kt, the green Flap 5 appears on the airspeed tape and Don commands 'Flap 5'.

The Captain moves the flap lever forward from 10° to five degrees and the EICAS display shows the flaps retracting to the new setting. When the flaps are retracted to five degrees, the fuel system automatically reconfigures once again. Crossfeed valves two and three open, allowing the centre tank or main wing tanks two and three to supply all engines, depending on the fuel load. On this flight, no fuel is being carried in the centre tank, so all the engines will draw from two and three main tanks. When all main tanks are equal in quantity, the system will be switched by the pilots to feed tank to engine.

ATC calls again.

**Toronto departure:** 'Air Canada eight five six heavy, turn right heading one zero zero.'

The new heading is dialled up and selected by the captain and the magenta bars of the flight

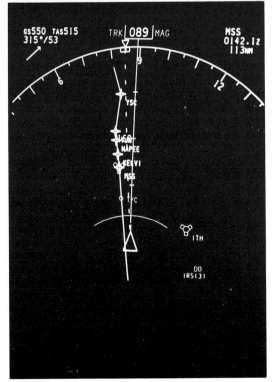

The ND during the climb out of Toronto. The arc crossing the track line indicates where the selected altitude will be reached. T/C, top of climb, marks the point where the final cruising altitude will be reached, barring any ATC restrictions. The distance and ETA to the next waypoint appear in the upper right. Groundspeed and true airspeed are displayed in the upper left along with the wind vector showing a wind speed of 53kt from 315°. The aircraft track line shows how the controller has taken the flight south of the flightplanned route.

```
FLIGHT AC0856/30    YYZ-LHR    FIN-342
TIME 01:12:27           DATE 93.07.01
-------------------------------------------
-//  TXN P111          01JUL/0112 YYZ1      C-GAGM/342/0856
 DFM AC856/30JUN YYZ 010112Z
FIN 342 DPKQ FOD 0166 ZFW 2393 ALTN GLA/      M860
YYZ 0057*01:07LA LHR 0717 00:52LE EQC 74E/16275 ----- -----
DL      PSN          ETO  F/L ATO  F/L EFOB AFOB PSN          AT  PSN
YYZ1    YYZ          0112 CLB          787
YOW1    MSS          0143 330          686
YFC1    MIILS        0218 330          612
YJT1    FROSS        0244 370          566
YAY1    DOTTY        0311 370          518
YAY1    52N50W       0334 370          478
        54N40W       0413 370          412
        55N30W       0449 370          349
        55N20W       0525 390          290
SNN1    55N10W       0603 390          229
DUB1    BEL          0618 390          205
DUB1    IOM          0659 370          194
LHR1    LHR          0700 370          166
```

**After take-off, a new flightplan with revised ETAs is received via ACARS.**

director command a turn to the right. The jet continues to accelerate and through 223kt, Flap 1 is selected. The trailing edge flaps move to one degree and the outboard leading edge flaps are retracted into the underside of the wing. On each wing there are 14 leading edge flaps; 11 variable camber flaps that are curved as they extend for take-off and landing, providing more efficient lift characteristics; and three Krueger flaps which are not curved and simply fold out as panels from beneath the inboard section of wing to extend the leading edge.

The aircraft's flight parallels the north shore of Lake Ontario and passengers on the right side of the aircraft are treated to a splendid view of Toronto. Set on the shore of the lake, the skyscrapers of the downtown core bask in the glow of the setting sun. Across the lake lies the Niagara Peninsula and Niagara Falls, a popular attraction for thousands of visitors each year. From this altitude, the lake's south shore and New York State are clearly visible. Passengers on the left side look down on the expanse of countryside dotted with many small lakes and rivers.

For the crew however, there's no time for sightseeing as ATC is calling again.

**Toronto departure:** 'Air Canada eight five six heavy, cleared to flight level two three oh.'

Bob selects 23,000ft in the altitude window and the climb continues. As the jet passes 242kt, the flap lever is moved to zero and the flaps are retracted. Below 10,000ft, aircraft are restricted to 250kt or less so the flight director command bars pitch up to keep the speed below the speed limit. It's 0116Z as the jet passes 5,800ft, climbing at 2,300ft per minute. With the aircraft cleaned up, it's time for the After Take-off checks. The runway turn-off and logo lights and inboard landing lights are checked off, the gear lever is moved to OFF and flaps are confirmed up. At 10,000ft, the seatbelt signs automatically go out and the outboard landing lights, which are left on at lower altitudes to make the jet more visible to other aircraft, are turned off by the crew. Smoking is not permitted on any of Air Canada's flights so the no-smoking sign is left on for the duration of the flight. Now above the speed restriction, the flight director allows the airspeed to build to a best climb speed just under 360kt.

Once the seatbelt signs have been extinguished, the flight attendants are able to get up and begin cabin service. Two flight attendants go through the cabin to ensure no passenger needs immediate assistance and then the beverage service is started.

Through 12,000ft, Don says 'Centre in Command' and Bob presses the button for the centre auto-pilot, activating one of three auto-pilots on the aircraft. The auto-pilot now takes over the task of flying the jet, maintaining the selected heading of 100° and continuing the climb to FL 230.

The departure controller calls again with a heading change to 090° and hands off Air Canada 856 to Toronto Centre on 127.0 MHz. Bob checks in and the centre controller clears the flight direct to MSS, the first waypoint. LNAV is selected and the auto-pilot will now fly the route input in the FMC. In fact, the FMS coupled with the auto-pilot could fly itself to Heathrow without any further actions by the pilots!

On the ND a track line stretches vertically across the screen, providing track guidance. A green arc intersecting the track line marks the point where the altitude selected in the auto-pilot will be reached. The top of climb marker, shown as T/C, appears further along the track line where the jet will reach final cruising altitude, barring any restrictions from ATC. In the upper right corner of the ND, MSS is displayed as the next waypoint with 197nm to go and an ETA of 0148Z.

Passing FL180, the altimeters are set to the standard pressure of 29.92 by pressing a selector on the mode control panel on the glareshield. The standard pressure is also set on the standby altimeter.

As the jet passes FL200, Don calls out an altitude check: 'twenty for twenty-three.'

When the gear lifted off the runway, the wheels-off time of 0112Z was automatically sent via ACARS to a computer in Air Canada's operations department. Using the actual departure time, the computer churned out a new flightplan with revised ETAs for the *en route* waypoints. Seconds later, the new flightplan rolls out of the printer on the centre console. As will soon be seen, the times are remarkably accurate.

With the revised times in hand, Don guards the ATC frequency while Bob dials up Gander Radio on the high frequency radio (HF). Tonight, he gets a response on the first try and the reception is crystal clear but that's not always the case with HF. High Frequency is used for long-distance communications and sometimes the atmospheric conditions can make transmissions unintelligible. That's why pilots are usually given a secondary frequency to try in the event communications are not possible on the primary. Gander ATC would have already received a copy of the flightplan for 856 some 10-12hr before departure outlining details of the flight such as aircraft type and the requested track, speed and altitude. Bob now provides Gander with the requested routeing for the North Atlantic crossing: Track Victor, FL370 at Mach 0.86, estimating DOTTY, the start of the crossing, at 0311Z. These details confirm the early flightplan received by Gander and help controllers as they organise the wave of evening flights converging on the oceanic control area. Now that controllers know what time Air Canada 856 will enter the OCA, they can look at other traffic that is expected at the same time and decide whether they can clear 856 as requested. Closer to the coast, the crew will pick up their actual clearance for the crossing.

While Bob was talking with Gander, Toronto Centre had called with clearance up to FL280 and requested a 20° right turn for vectors to MSS. The heading change takes the aircraft south of the direct track to MSS and is likely required for spacing because of other aircraft in the area. As suspected, it becomes apparent that the controller is trying to organise a stream of eastbound aircraft.

**Toronto Centre:** 'Air Canada eight five six heavy will you be able Flight Level three seven oh today? I've got a couple of aircraft overhead you at Flight Level three three oh so it might be better for you.'

The crew find out from the controller that the only way they will be able to get their initial requested altitude of FL330 is to restrict their speed to Mach 0.83. That would cost fuel so the pilots decide on the higher altitude where they will be able to cruise at Mach 0.86 unrestricted. A check of the FMC performance page confirms that at the current weight, the aircraft is able to reach FL370.

The controller clears the crew to FL310 and advises that they can expect higher in several miles. Sure enough, after a short time, ATC is calling with further clearance.

**Toronto Centre:** 'Air Canada eight five six heavy cleared to maintain flight level three seven oh and heading of zero eight five. When out of flight level three five oh, direct Massena on course.'

Approaching FL350, Air Canada 856 must be past the other traffic since the controller calls and clears the crew direct to MSS before handing them off to Montreal Centre on 134.4 MHz. Checking in with Montreal Centre, the controller clears them direct MIILS. On the legs page of the FMC, MIILS is selected to the top of the waypoint list. The FMC treats the change as a revision to the original flightplan and displays it as a modified route until the pilots press the Execute button and the amendment becomes the active route.

In the climb, the aircraft bumps through some light chop. Bob reports the turbulence to the controller so that he can pass it on to other flights who may want the information.

At 0137Z, the aircraft reaches its cruising altitude of 37,000ft. The climb has taken 25min and covered just under 200nm. The throttles automatically retard to maintain the selected cruise speed and the upper EICAS shows the engines have settled into cruise at 1.38 EPR, 90.6% N1 and an EGT of 417° Celsius. The jet is flying at Mach 0.856, slightly less than the selected cruise of Mach 0.86. The true airspeed, compensated for altitude and temperature, is 506kt. The wind vector on the ND shows the wind at this altitude is 309° at 65kt, giving a ground speed of 546kt.

Once level, the crew run through the cruise check which is a general scan of the flightdeck instrumentation to ensure that all the switches are properly set.

Now clear of the busy terminal areas and level at the cruising altitude, the crew can settle into a routine for the cruise portion of the flight. Ahead lies the Atlantic. London is 5hr 20min away.

# En Route

Flying some seven miles high, the only sensation of movement comes from the steady roar — not of the engines — but of the thin air as it rushes past the nose of the aircraft. By now, the sun has set and the western sky is aglow in shades of orange and red. The twinkling pattern of lights of towns and cities look like islands in the darkness, connected by thin ribbons of roads with tiny car headlights visible. The sprawl of Montreal passes on the left, partially hidden by a thin layer of cloud which glows from the city lights beneath. The majestic St Lawrence River stretches off to the northeast. The cockpit itself is dark and the pilots' faces are highlighted by the glow of the CRTs and instrumentation.

Winking strobe lights below and to the left mark the position of an aircraft climbing east-bound out of Montreal. Aircraft are illuminated at night in the same way as boats with a green light on the starboard or right wing, a red light on the port side and a white light on the tail. ('Red the sailor left port' is a saying that serves as a reminder that red is left which is port.) The aircraft is also equipped with anti-collision lights: brilliant white strobes lights flash on each wingtip and the tail and two flashing red strobes on the top and belly of the fuselage make the jet more visible to other aircraft in the vicinity.

When aircraft are spotted at night, the arrangement of lights enables pilots to tell almost immediately the other aircraft's direction of travel and whether there is potential for conflict. For instance, if the crew spot green and red lights ahead of them that are not moving in relation to their own aircraft they know that there is the possibility of a head-on collision unless evasive action is taken.

It's 0145Z and the flight is handed over to Montreal Centre on 132.55 MHz. The light chop that had jiggled the flight during the last stages of the climb has smoothed out and Bob passes that on to the controller. Using ACARS, Don requests the current weather for London and less than a minute later, the weather report curls out of the printer. London is reporting CAVOK (Ceiling and Visibility Okay) and a temperature 18° Celsius and it's still the middle of the night. It promises to be a hot day in the city.

The radio crackles as ATC calls with a frequency change. Bob checks in with Boston Centre on 128.05.

**Captain R/T:** 'Boston Centre, it's Air Canada eight five six heavy, three seven oh.'

The controller responds with a simple acknowledgement and the routine of cruise continues. Several minutes pass when a single chime sounds in the cockpit. It's the Flight Service Director calling on the intercom, telling the flight crew that if they wish to speak to the passengers, now is a good opportunity. The flight attendants will often keep the pilots informed about the progress of cabin service so they can pick a good time to talk on the PA and avoid interrupting a movie. Don picks up the PA handset from the rear of the centre console and takes a few moments to fill the passengers in on the flight's progress.

**First Officer PA:** 'Good evening ladies and gentlemen, first officer speaking. Currently at 37,000ft *en route* to London Heathrow. We just passed Montreal seven minutes ago and will be making our departure from Canada just to the north of St John's, Newfoundland, and from there across the North Atlantic at 55° north. We'll be making our landfall over Belfast on the other side and from there across the Irish Sea and on into London. Due to our late departure time our arrival time in London will be 10min past eight. For those of you who wish to change your watches, it is now three-oh-six in the morning. Looking for a lovely day in London, calling for sunny skies, light winds and a temperature high of 28° Celsius. Thank you.'

As Montreal passes behind, the pace slackens considerably, giving the pilots their first opportunity to sit back and relax since the busy departure. At this point, the onboard computers and auto-pilot are doing everything: navigating to MIILS with the nose of the aircraft crabbed slightly to the right to offset the effects of wind; regulating the temperature throughout the cabin; and monitoring engine performance. The control columns move slightly as the auto-pilot makes corrections to keep the jet on course. The aircraft systems have been designed to 'set and forget' before take-off and require little attention during the flight. Indeed, there's an old joke that with all the automation, the aircraft of tomorrow will be crewed by a Captain and a Dobermann Pinscher. The Captain's job will be to feed the dog. And the dog is there to bite the Captain if he attempts to touch anything.

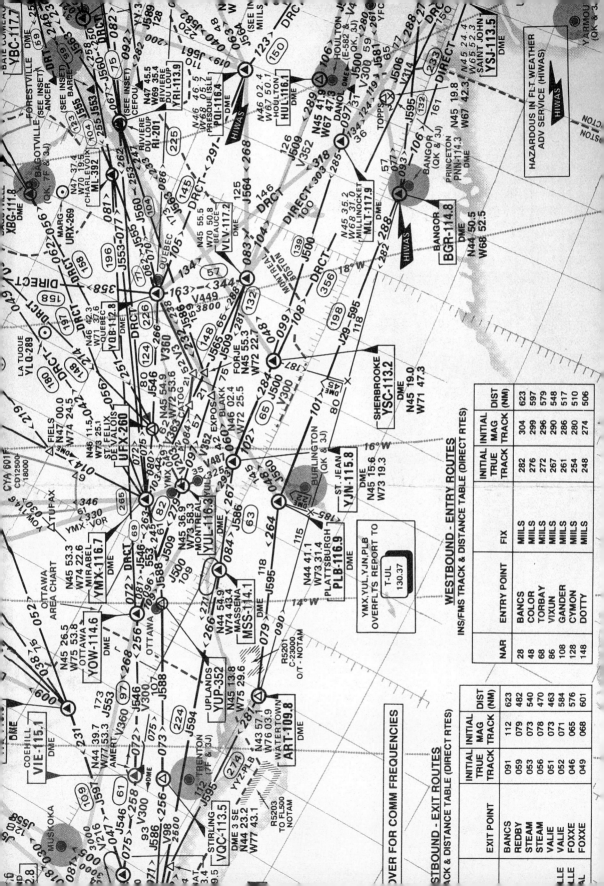

*Left:*
**Section of the high altitude chart showing part of the route from Toronto to DOTTY.** *Air Canada*

Even though the actual physical task of flying the aircraft across the Atlantic will be handled by the auto-pilot, the pilots are carefully monitoring the flight and engine displays, ready to take over at the first sign that something is amiss. Some emergencies require immediate actions that are performed by the crew from memory. But once those are completed, the pilots pull out the emergency and abnormal procedure checklist to ensure the problem has been properly dealt with. Unlike emergencies experienced at take-off, which require quick action, the handling of malfunctions *en route* can be discussed and pondered and the best option chosen. The last thing the pilots want to do is to make a difficult situation worse because of a hasty action. When dealing with any sort of problem, safety is the number one priority for the crew. But, depending on the seriousness of the situation, other factors such as the availability of maintenance crews and the inconvenience to the passengers play a role in what the crew decides to do next and even where they decide to divert to.

Boeing has revised the cockpit procedures on the -400 to reflect the fact that two crew are doing the work rather than three. The checklist items for normal procedures have been reduced from 107 on the 747-200/300 to just 34 on the -400. Emergency procedures have also been revised to minimise the pilots' duties during a crisis and can be done by one pilot. For instance, the checklist for a rapid decompression and emergency descent on the Boeing checklist for the -400 has just three items on it, compared to 20 on the earlier 747 models; the checklist to handle a trip of an air-conditioning pack has two items, down from 11. (The actual number of procedures can vary from airline to airline.)

Fire is the most serious threat to aircraft, particularly on long over-water legs when it could take several hours to reach an airport for an emergency landing. For that reason, the aft and forward cargo compartments are equipped with smoke detectors and an extinguishing system that can flood the compartment with Halon, an inert gas, for a minimum of 180min to keep a cargo fire under control until the aircraft can fly to an airport and land. And the 747-400 requires just two actions for a cargo fire, compared to 16 on previous models. The main deck cargo compartment is similarly equipped with smoke detectors and fire extinguishers that are controlled from the flightdeck. When the guarded switch on the overhead panel is lifted and pushed, four bottles of extinguisher are discharged initially to flood the compartment to a five per cent minimum Halon concentration. The remaining three bottles are discharged after an eight-minute delay to extend the time to a minimum of 20min of fire protection. This allows a crew member to don a fire suit, enter the compartment and fight the fire. Each Combi flight is required to have at least one flight attendant trained in fire-fighting techniques.

The procedures to deal with an engine fire have been cut as well to just four on the -400 compared with 15 on the -200 and -300. In the event of an engine fire, a loud gong sounds in the cockpit, a red fire warning appears on the EICAS and the red master warning light on the glareshield goes on. As well, the appropriate fire control lever on the overhead panel and the fuel cut-off switch behind the throttles are illuminated in red. The handles are normally locked in position to prevent an inadvertent engine or APU shutdown and are released when a fire is detected. Pulling out the fire handle shuts down the engine, closes the fuel valve, trips the electric generator field, closes the bleed air and hydraulic valves and arms the extinguisher bottle. After the fire handle is pulled, it can be rotated left or right to discharge the extinguisher. Two fire bottles are installed in each wing leading edge, just inboard of the inboard engine, and are piped to supply both engines on that side of the aircraft. The fire extinguisher is designed to flood the engine cowling with Halon. If the fire light remains illuminated 30sec after the first bottle is discharged, the fire handle is turned to discharge the remaining extinguisher bottle.

Although such in-flight emergencies are rare, the crews are trained to handle any occurrence and regularly attend rigorous refresher sessions to hone their skills. Four times a year, each pilot is required to show his or her proficiency at safely handling the aircraft under a variety of gruelling emergency and unusual conditions. Such emergencies include engine failures near V1 on take-off, two and three engine landings in bad weather and failures of various aircraft systems. Obviously, these situations could never be safely practised in a real aircraft so airlines rely on sophisticated simulators that duplicate the flightdeck with surprising realism. Computer graphics create day- and night-time images outside the cockpit windows and the whole machine moves about on hydraulic jacks, capturing the sensations of flight to the point that first-time visitors can experience feelings of queasiness.

In fact simulators today are so advanced that pilots can do all their training without ever leaving the ground. The conversion course for Air Canada pilots upgrading to the -400 takes about two months and includes three weeks of ground

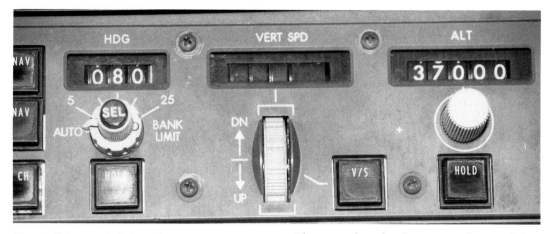

**The auto-flight controls during cruise.**

school, 20hr in a fixed base simulator that duplicates the flightdeck environment without the motion and 40hr in the full motion simulator. Their first flight at the controls of a -400 is on a revenue flight under the supervision of a check pilot or instructor.

Air Canada does not have a -400 simulator of its own so the airline's pilots travel to Minneapolis, Minnesota, twice a year to train on a simulator owned by Northwest Airlines. Each two-day trip consists of a four-hour practice session with an instructor and a four-hour session that is graded by a check pilot. In addition to the proficiency checks, the pilots must also pass route checks and rigorous medical examinations to make sure they are fit to fly. All these checks combine to make a professional pilot one of the most scrutinised professionals in the world.

A knock on the flightdeck door interrupts the quiet interlude and a flight attendant enters. She brings a dish of nuts and a welcome cup of coffee for the Captain and a glass of ice for the First Officer which he tops up from a bottle of water he keeps at his side. The crew drink regularly to offset the effects of the dry cabin air.

By this point, the passengers have enjoyed a short news programme and a 40min broadcast touching on current affairs, people and destinations, both shown on overhead video screens throughout the cabin. The cabin crew are just finishing the meal service. Depending on the flight, passengers in Hospitality Class usually have their choice of tasty beef or chicken dishes. The service in First and Business classes is quite elaborate with a wide choice of meals and beverages offered to the passengers. Travellers on religious or medical diets can request speciality meals, such as vegetarian, Hindu or diabetic, when booking their ticket.

Dinner service takes just over an hour and then it is time for the feature movie, which, on this flight, is entitled *Enchanted April*.

MIILS is passed at 0219Z and the big jet turns towards FROSS which is 239nm away and should be reached at 0245Z. A check of the wind vector on the ND shows the winds are blowing from 289° at 66kt and fuel remaining on board is 62,700kg, a healthy 4,500kg over the flightplan. At each waypoint, the flight's progress and the fuel load are noted on the flight log and compared against the estimates. It's not uncommon to encounter lighter than normal tailwinds or headwinds which impact upon the flight's fuel consumption. The pilots must ensure that sufficient reserves will be on board on arrival in case of a diversion for bad weather. If calculations show the fuel burn is higher than forecast, a landing *en route* might be required to take on additional fuel. The crew also compare the time and distance to the next way-

**The CDU display showing the flight's fuel state.**

# DINNER

Hot Hors d'oeuvres

Fresh Russian Sevruga Caviar

Smoked Quail with Celery and Orange Salad
Terrine of Duck Liver

Vichyssoise

Roast Rack of Lamb with Rosemary
or
Lobster with Whisky Sauce
or
Vegetarian Plate

Bouquetière of Vegetables

Seasonal Salad

Selection of Cheese and Fresh Fruit

Hazelnut Cake
Lemon Sherbet

Coffee, Decaffeinated Coffee, Tea, Herbal Tea

---

*A sumptuous cold platter
is also available at your leisure.*

# BREAKFAST

Orange Juice

Yogurt

Fresh Fruit

Soft-boiled Eggs prepared to your taste

Bread Basket, Marmalade, Jam, Honey

*Above:*
**Since the time of writing, the first class service has been replaced by Executive First, an upgraded business service, located in the forward cabin of the 747-400.**

*Middle:*
**Engine indications during cruise show on EICAS.**

*Left:*
**The first class menu.** *Air Canada*

55

Dawn breaks over the North Atlantic, bathing the flightdeck in bright sunlight.

point as shown on the ND against the figures in the flightplan to ensure there is no discrepancy — yet another check to guard against errors. The regime of checks and doublechecks is particularly important on a two-pilot flightdeck since there isn't the insurance of the third pair of eyes looking on. Air Canada was among the airlines that pioneered the use of extended range operations for the Boeing 767 and, along with it, developed the standards for two-crew cockpits that became the foundation for procedures at several other airlines.

At each oceanic waypoint, the pilots also check the accuracy of each IRU and ensure none of the three units are displaying a position markedly different from the others. However, the reliability of the units today makes even small errors uncommon. The airspace over the North Atlantic between FL275 and FL400 stretching from the North Pole to 27° North forms the North Atlantic Minimum Navigation Performance Specifications area. Under standards adopted world-wide, aircraft flying in this airspace, which include virtually all transatlantic flights, must be equipped with navigation equipment that can accurately track the aircraft's position. This is to ensure that the aircraft are established on the tracks and maintaining the proper lateral distances from other aircraft.

ATC responsibility for the flight is handed over to Moncton Centre on 132.7 and the pilots tune in to hear the controller asking the crew of a Continental flight to check if they can hear an Emergency Locator Transmitter (ELT) on the emergency frequency of 121.5. ELTs are carried by all aircraft and are automatically activated in a crash, emitting a distinctive warbling signal to help search teams home in on the wreckage.

It's 0226Z as Chatham, New Brunswick, passes under the nose. The flight is over the Maritime Provinces and the start of the Atlantic crossing is less than an hour away.

Two minutes later, the flight's oceanic clearance sent via datalink from Gander rolls out of the printer on the centre console. Datalinks are used by pilots to communicate primarily with airline operations on subjects like maintenance problems that need repair upon the aircraft's arrival. But in what promises to be the way of the future, Gander is using datalink to transmit oceanic clearances to some flights. In fact, Air Canada was the first airline in the world to receive an ATC clearance via datalink. It's unlikely this will ever replace voice communications for air traffic control but the system is perfectly suited for tasks such as clearance delivery, when the reading of clearances can tie up radio frequencies. And by providing pilots with a written copy of a clearance, it eliminates the ambiguity and confusion caused by accents or poor radio reception. The datalinks transmit on VHF but the future use of satellites could enable communications with airline operations and ATC in areas where VHF reception is now poor or impossible, like the middle of the ocean.

The clearance shows that Air Canada 856 has been cleared as filed: Track Victor, FL370 at Mach 0.86. The pilots compare the routeing as spelled out in the clearance against what was entered in the FMC and it checks out okay.

Approaching the border of the oceanic zone, the workload starts to pick up. At 0228Z, it's time for another frequency change and Bob checks in with the next Moncton sector on 132.8. The distinctive wail of an ELT is heard on the emergency frequency of 121.5 which has been tuned on the right VHF. The ELT signal is very strong but intermittent. This is reported to ATC to help give authorities some idea of the ELT's location. The source of this mystery will go unsolved since it's not long before the wail fades out. Bob and Don decide to ask ATC if they can proceed direct to DOTTY, which would save a few minutes.

**Captain R/T:** 'Air Canada eight five six requesting direct to Dotty.'
**Moncton Centre:** 'Air Canada eight five six, cleared as requested.'

The Captain reaches down to the CDU, selects DOTTY as the next waypoint and activates the amended flightplan. Obediently, the aircraft turns to a heading of 080° to fly direct to DOTTY. Looking out the front windows, the wingtip strobe lights of two aircraft likely headed overseas as well can be seen flashing in the darkness ahead.

The flight isn't long with Moncton before it's over to Gander Centre on 133.55. Bob checks in with Gander and is immediately asked to call Gander clearance on 135.05 to confirm details of the oceanic clearance. While Don stays on the air traffic control frequency, Bob dials up Gander clearance.

**Captain R/T:** 'Gander, it's Air Canada eight five six.'
**Gander R/T:** 'Air Canada eight five six, standby.'

The reason for the controller's request is soon apparent — Caledonian Airways, Virgin, American and several other airlines are trying to squeeze a word in edgeways on the busy frequency to get their oceanic clearances. Air Canada 856 has arrived at the oceanic boundary during the busiest time for eastbound flights. Airlines in North America schedule their flights to Europe to depart in the evening and arrive at the start of the following day. The result is a rush of eastbound flights from Miami, New York, Chicago, Toronto and other North American airports that starts at 0100Z and tapers off around 0600Z. During the busiest three to four hours, Gander controllers handle 75-80 flights an hour, integrating the aircraft into oceanic airspace and ensuring proper separation as they start across the ocean. The non-stop chatter on the frequency is a perfect example of how clearances delivered by datalink could bring some relief to the congestion.

It's not long before the controller is calling Air Canada 856. Normally if a clearance has already been received via datalink, the pilot has only to read back the number of the clearance. However, this time, the controller wants the full read-back so the Captain complies.

**Captain R/T:** 'We're cleared to London via Dotty, track Victor fifty-two fifty, fifty-four forty, fifty-five thirty, fifty-five twenty, fifty-five ten, Belfast, three seven zero, Mach eight six.'
**Gander R/T:** 'Air Canada eight five six, read-back is correct, return to your last assigned control frequency now, good-night.'

Bob calls Gander Centre and advises that the flight has received its oceanic clearance. The ND shows the aircraft will reach DOTTY, 230nm away, at 0314Z. The wind has swung around to 271° at 44kt and to make good the track of 082° to DOTTY, the auto-pilot has settled on a heading of 096° to counter the effects of wind.

With just minutes to go before reaching the border of the oceanic control area, Gander Centre

The Captain's PFD and ND during cruise. The PFD shows an IAS of 283kt level at 37,000. The selected cruise speed of Mach 0.865 is seen at the top of the airspeed tape and the actual cruise speed of Mach 0.863 at the bottom.

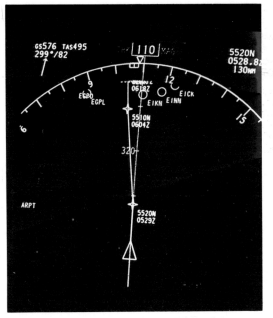

**The ND range is set to 640nm and at the top of the display, circles appear marking the location of Irish airports, indicating that the ocean crossing is nearly over.**

takes a position report and asks the crew to call Gander Radio on HF primary 2899 or secondary 5616. Position reports received by the radio operators with the Gander International Flight Service Station are automatically passed by computer to controllers in the Gander Oceanic Control sector, which oversees flights to 30 West, the mid-point of the ocean. Bob tunes Gander Radio on the HF frequency and asks for a Selcal check. Selcal (Selective Calling System) is a device that allows ATC to alert a crew if they wish to make contact. Each aircraft has its own unique Selcal code, like DP-KQ which has been assigned to C-CAGM, enabling ground stations to ring individual aircraft. The system saves the pilots from keeping a listening watch to the static on HF for the duration of the crossing.

**Captain R/T:** 'Gander, requesting Selcal check Delta Papa Kilo Quebec.'

Seconds later, the request is rewarded by a two-tone chime that sounds on the flightdeck. Bob confirms to the radio operator that the check was okay and the crew now remove their headsets, knowing that ATC can reach them if needed.

At 0320Z, Air Canada 856 passes DOTTY, an imaginary waypoint located just south of St Anthony's on the northern tip of the island of Newfoundland. It has taken three hours — just less than half the journey — to reach Canada's eastern border, a testament to the country's vast expanse. Ahead lies some 2,000nm of ocean before landfall over Ireland. The jet is about to leave Canada. However, the event goes unnoticed in the cabin — for passengers, their departure from Canada happened at the airport.

Below is Newfoundland. Located at the eastern-most edge of North America, the island was for so long the ideal springboard for transatlantic flights. Yet those early flyers still had the expanse of unpredictable ocean to cross — some flights ended in success, others in tragedy. The distinction of being the first to cross the Atlantic non-stop goes to Capt John Alcock and Lt Arthur Whitten Brown who made the trip in a Vickers Vimy twin-engined bomber. On 14 June 1919, the heavily laden biplane staggered into the air from a field in Newfoundland. Battling cold, icing, fog and turbulence, the crew put their plane down in a peat bog in County Galway in Ireland, 16hr 30min after they set out.

Others would follow. Charles Lindbergh flew from New York to Paris in May 1927, making him the first to fly the Atlantic solo. In 1932, Amelia Earhart became the first woman to fly the Atlantic solo, starting from Newfoundland and landing in Londonderry, Northern Ireland. These were daring flights that made the front page of newspapers around the world and made heroes out of the pilots. Yet the passengers on tonight's flight likely won't give a second thought to those early flights

**Back in radio range, the Captain uses ACARS to get weather reports for Heathrow (LHR), Goose Bay, Newfoundland (YYR), Shannon (SNN), and Glasgow (GLA).**

```
FLIGHT AC0856/30    YYZ-LHR    FIN-342
TIME 06:00:56          DATE 93.07.01
----------------------------------------
-// WXX P123            01JUL/0600 SNN1      C-GAGM/    /0856
  ;AWDSA/M/LHR/YYR/SNN/GLA                                      93/07/01  06:00
LHR   SA 010000 2350 02002KT CAVOK 18/12 1018 NOSIG
YYR   SA 010500 90 SCT 250 -SCT 15 113/9/6/1906/986/AC1CI1 /BLUE/ 2124
SNN   SA
AW0030: NO CURRENT WX
GLA   SA 010500 0520 24006KT 9999 SCT012 09/07 Q1021 NOSIG
...END
```

as they sip their coffees, adjust their headphones and settle in to watch a movie — at 37,000ft.

Sitting on the flightdeck of the 747-400, the advances are not lost on the Captain or the First Officer, both of whom have seen dramatic strides in aviation during their time as pilots. Bob started with the airline in 1956 on the DC-3 and over the years has flown the DC-4, Viscount, Vanguard, Boeing 727, 747 and 767 before transitioning to the 747-400. His first Atlantic crossing was in a DC-8 and in those days, transatlantic flights were manned by a Captain, First Officer, Second Officer, and navigator.

Bob originally wanted to be a train engineer but credits his mother who had the foresight to see the growth in aviation. But he didn't lose his interest in trains. He is one of several avid volunteers who devote their spare time to running a 110-year old steam engine. In fact, Bob is likely one of the few people in the world 'dual rated' to pilot the sophisticated 747-400 and drive an 1883 coal-fired steam locomotive.

Don joined the airline in 1967 after serving seven years in the air force, flying Sabre jet fighters in Europe and instructing on Chipmunks in Ontario. He started on the Vanguard, served as a Second Officer for a time on the DC-8 and went on to fly the DC-9, 727, L-1011 and the 747 'Classic' which he flew for six years.

With the workload of entering the oceanic control area behind them and the jet cruising smoothly, the pilots settle into a quiet routine that will mark the flight until the ocean crossing is completed in roughly three hours. During this time, they update their chart books, do some paperwork and get up for a few moments to stretch their legs although one pilot must remain at the controls at all times to monitor the aircraft and handle any emergencies should they arise.

Air Canada 856 has slowly caught up to one of the aircraft that was seen ahead earlier and it passes under the nose, 2,000ft below on the same track. Sensing the other aircraft below, the radio altimeter on the PFD flickers briefly to 2,000ft as the -400 passes directly overhead — a dramatic demonstration of the accuracy of the Inertial Reference System.

The IRS consists of three individual initial reference units (IRUs). Each IRU contains three ring laser gyros and three accelerometers. These units measure the smallest movements and accelerations which are combined with air data inputs to provide a variety of information such as attitude, latitude and longitude, true and magnetic headings, wind speed and direction and vertical speed.

Unlike the earlier electro-mechanical gyros used for INS, the laser gyros have no spinning parts, providing high reliability and tremendous accuracy. After an ocean crossing, it wasn't uncommon for the INS to be out 10-12nm, compared to the IRS which is out only marginally, if at all. With previous navigation systems, aircraft were often spotted close to, but not directly on the oceanic tracks. However with IRS, the aircraft are dead centre on track, flying accurately on course.

Yet, for all the sophistication of the onboard navigation equipment, separation of aircraft over the North Atlantic is still based on the age-old tenets of air traffic control — time and distance. Since radar coverage extends only about 200nm from land, air traffic controllers rely on pilots' position reports to keep track of traffic over the ocean and ensure that adequate separation is being maintained. On the tracks, aircraft are separated vertically by 2,000ft or laterally by time. Aircraft operating on the same track at the same altitude at the same speed are separated by 10min. That can be reduced to a minimum of five minutes if the first aircraft is faster than the one behind. If the faster aircraft is behind other traffic on the same track at the same altitude, controllers must apply greater separation to ensure that there is a minimum of 10min between the two aircraft when they enter European domestic radar coverage after the crossing.

**The First Officer runs through the approach briefing and the crew prepare for the arrival in London.**

Airlines and government officials are studying several options that could reduce the required separation on the North Atlantic and ease congestion. The first would reduce vertical separation on the tracks to 1,000ft. The other option looks to the heavens and satellites. Position reports fed from aircraft to air traffic control via satellites could enable ATC to develop a synthetic radar picture of traffic on the North Atlantic and allow reduced lateral separations.

For now though, those advances are still years away and air traffic control continues to rely on position reports that have been filed by pilots since the early days of ocean flying.

At 0336Z, Bob reaches to the edge of the glareshield and turns on his overhead map light which casts a small pool on to his lap and illuminates the flight log. The flight has just passed 5250N and it's time to file a position report with Gander Radio on HF. The jet has burned 31,300kg, leaving 48,900kg.

Since the jet is racing eastward, it will be a short night and already the eastern horizon is beginning to soften. The horizon to the north glows bright where the Arctic is enjoying 24hr of summer sun. Looking out the port side windows, the darkness overhead is broken by the twinkling of aurora borealis, or northern lights. Pilots are often treated to dazzling displays of the eerie lights caused by electrical discharges 60-200 miles up in the Earth's atmosphere.

Thirty minutes after entering the oceanic control area, the jet is beyond radar coverage and code 2000 is selected on the transponder. The pilots leave the emergency frequency tuned on the right VHF and the air-to-air frequency of 131.8 is dialled up on the left VHF. Airlines might be fiercely competitive on the ground but it's a different story in the air. This frequency is used by pilots over the Atlantic to share important flight information like areas of turbulence as well as to banter and pass the time.

The message 'ACARS NO COMM' has appeared on the upper EICAS to inform the pilots that

**Preparing breakfast in the galley on the upper deck.**

ACARS is unusable since the flight is beyond VHF range. That message is joined by another alerting the pilots that the fuel load is now equal in the wing tanks. Don responds by turning off crossfeed valves one and four and the override jettison fuel pumps. The boost pumps now provide a tank to engine feed for the remainder of the flight.

At 0352Z, a check of the ND shows the wind is 275 at 87kt, giving a healthy ground speed of 583kt. With its cruise speed of Mach 0.86, the 747-400 is one of the fastest jets on the North Atlantic and routinely overtakes 767s, which cruise at Mach 0.82, and the 747 'Classics' at Mach 0.84. In scheduled service, the -400 has shaved five minutes off the Toronto-London route previously flown by a 'Classic'. The difference is even more pronounced on westbound trips against prevailing winds where the -400 makes the trip 15min faster.

5440N passes under the aircraft symbol on the ND and it's time for another position report.

**Captain R/T:** 'Gander, it's Air Canada eight five six. Fifty-four north, forty west, zero four one six, estimating fifty-five north, thirty west at zero four five three. Fifty-five north, twenty west next. Fuel on board forty-two point three. Gander copy Shannon.'

Wisps of cloud, barely visible in the pre-dawn darkness, stream past the windows as the jet flies along the top of a thin layer of cirrus cloud, giving some sensation of the aircraft's speed. A flight attendant pops into the flightdeck to ask if either pilot is interested in supper. Bob declines, saying he grabbed dinner before the flight, but the First Officer elects to try a pasta dish. Rules require that the Captain and First Officer eat different meals cooked in separate ovens to avoid the possibility of incapacitation by food poisoning.

There is now little over three hours left in the journey and with dinner dishes cleared away, the crew welcome their first visitors, a group of children who are ushered in by a flight attendant. A visit to the flightdeck is a popular highlight of any flight, especially for children, and the pilots try to accommodate the requests whenever the workload permits. The stream of visitors continues non-stop as the pilots explain the flightdeck workings to the wide-eyed youngsters, including one boy who compares the CRT displays to his $100 handheld computer game.

The horizon begins to redden with the approach of daybreak. Darkness still shrouds the ocean but even during daytime flights there is little to see apart from a carpet of white cloud, patches of water and the glimpse of an occasional iceberg. Nearing 30 West, the flight passes the equal fuel point. If an emergency occurs now and a diversion becomes necessary, the crew will head to Shannon rather than return to Gander. Thirty west is crossed shortly after and responsibility for the flight passes to Shanwick    the radio operators are stationed near Shannon, Ireland, and the control centre is in Prestwick.

**Captain R/T:** 'Shanwick, it's Air Canada eight five six.'

**Shanwick R/T:** 'Air Canada eight five six, Shanwick.'

**Captain R/T:** 'Air Canada eight five six is at five five north, three zero west at zero four five three, flight level three seven zero, estimating five five north two zero west at zero five two nine. Five five north one zero west is next, fuel on board is three six decimal three.'

**Shanwick radio:** 'You're quite weak sir. Air Canada eight five six Shanwick confirm, copy Gander. Five five north, three zero west zero four five three. Three seven zero. Five five north, twenty west at zero five three niner. Five five north, one zero west. Three six decimal three on the fuel. Is that affirmative?'

**Captain R/T:** 'Just the five five north, two zero west time. It should be zero five two nine. Copy that.'

**Shanwick radio:** 'Zero five two niner, roger. But just for a radio check could you call me on 8864?'

Bob calls on the other frequency and finding reception somewhat clearer, goes through the routine of getting a Selcal check. The jet turns to a heading of 108° for 5520N, 335nm away. Dawn breaks on the North Atlantic shortly after 0500Z, revealing a thick layer of clouds below that are part of a weather system that will bring showers to the British Isles in the days to come. Sunlight floods the flightdeck and the pilots position glareshields over the front windows to reduce some of the glare. The Captain's ND is set to 640nm and at the upper edge of the display, several blue circles appear marking the position of Irish airports. The night-time hours of the crossing always seem to crawl by but daybreak and the brogue of the radio operator make London seem close at hand. With the coast of the Emerald Isle less than one hour's flying time away, the ocean crossing is nearly over and the crew turn their thoughts to the arrival in London.

Approaching from the north, it's likely the flight will be routed into Heathrow via BNN, the Bovingdon VOR, for a landing on Runway 27 Right. The First Officer enters details of the Bovingdon Standard Terminal Arrival Route into the FMC which automatically computes the points to start

descents and slow down to meet altitude and speed restrictions. Reading from the approach plate for the ILS 27 Right, Don tunes the outer marker ADF frequency of 389.5 and the ILS frequency of 110.3 in the FMC. Using a yellow highlighter pen, he marks the important heights on the approach chart.

A check of the FMC shows that the flight's optimum cruise altitude is 36,800ft, just less than the current cruise. The computer also informs the pilots that if an engine failed, the aircraft would be able to maintain a maximum of 34,600ft.

Just prior to 5520N, the flight encounters some light turbulence (it must be time for breakfast!) and the Captain reaches up and turns on the continuous ignition to the engines to minimise any chance of a flame-out.

5520N is passed at 0528Z and the aircraft turns slightly right for the final leg of the North Atlantic route to 5510N which lies 344nm away and should be crossed at 0604Z. Approaching 15 West, the flight is likely back within radar range although the flight will remain with Shanwick oceanic control until 10 West is reached.

As the fuel load has burned off during cruise, the auto-throttles have gradually reduced the engine thrust needed to keep the selected cruise speed.

At 0536Z, a message flashes on the upper EICAS display, directing the pilots' attention to the lower EICAS display where the secondary engine information has appeared automatically. The oil quantity for one engine is low at four litres but the oil pressure and temperature are normal and suggest nothing is amiss. The quantity jumps to five litres and a few minutes later, the lower EICAS goes blank — the oil level has apparently returned to normal. Though there doesn't appear to have been anything wrong, it's a good demonstration of how the computerised flightdeck alerts the pilots to potential problems.

At 0555Z, the aircraft is back within VHF range and the Captain uses ACARS to request weather reports for Heathrow and the alternate airports Glasgow and Shannon. The reports are received in short order and show clear weather all around.

Approaching 5510N at 0605Z, the crew bid goodbye to Shanwick and tune Scottish Control on 135.85 and are rewarded with clearance direct IOM, a VOR located at the tip of the Isle of Man. The flight has entered its final leg and the sights and sounds of London are just over an hour away.

**The ND during the last stages of cruise shows the jet over the Wallasey VOR and about to turn towards HON, a VOR southeast of Birmingham. T/D on the track line marks the Top of Descent point where the jet should start its descent.**

# Arrival

The cloud cover that masked the ocean has melted away, providing passengers on both sides of the aircraft with a picture postcard view of Ireland and the country's unmistakable patchwork quilt of green fields visible even from 37,000ft. It's certainly not a view the Captain gets to enjoys every morning for breakfast as he uses the last few quiet minutes of cruise to nibble on a tasty snack of a boiled egg, sweet bun, yogurt and some fruit.

Contact is established with airline staff in London via ACARS and from them it's learned that Runway 9 Left will probably be the landing runway. This unravels some of the earlier preparation that had been done by the First Officer. Bob pulls out his chartbook once again, this time selecting the ILS 9 Left approach plate. The majority of approaches to the world's major airports are done using an electronic aid called the Instrument Landing System (ILS). The system consists of two separate radio signals; a localiser antenna located at the far end of the runway sends out a signal guiding aircraft along the centreline of the runway. A separate glideslope antenna guides aircraft along an even rate of descent, usually a three degree glideslope, to the runway. Don tunes the ILS frequency of 110.3 in the FMC and dials up the Minimum Descent Altitude (MDA) of 280ft on the PFD. The MDA marks the lowest altitude an aircraft can descend to during an instrument approach without seeing the ground. If the ground is not visible by this point, a go-around must be initiated.

Today, however, the crew have elected to let the auto-pilots do the landing at Heathrow. Although it's certainly not required with the clear weather, the pilots like to do the occasional autoland for practice and to test the systems. The Boeing 747-400 is equipped with a very sophisticated package of three auto-pilots able to land the big jet in 'blind' conditions of dense fog. Air Canada pilots are qualified to make landings with virtually no decision height and a runway visual range of 150ft. During landings in such conditions, the pilots will maybe see one or two runway lights and often won't see the runway at all until after touchdown. On days like those, taxying to the terminal in such limited visibility is often the toughest thing about the arrival.

Together the two pilots run through the approach briefing, highlighting the critical altitudes and what actions will be taken in the event of a go-around.

**First Officer:** 'This is an ILS approach on zero nine left. Twenty five hundred (Initial approach altitude), twenty-five hundred (Glidepath intercept altitude) and twelve thirty (altitude over the outer marker). Decision height is two hundred and eighty. Call one hundred above and minimum and I'll call landing or go-around. In the event of a go-around, it's climb straight ahead to three thousand then as directed by ATC. In the event of a missed approach, I'll call go-around. I'll press the go-around switch, ensure the throttles are moving up, call for flaps twenty.'

**Captain:** 'I'll select flap twenty and say positive rate.'

**First Officer:** 'I'll call for gear up and missed approach altitude set. At four hundred feet I'll call for LNAV and at six hundred feet, I'll call for VNAV. And at a thousand feet, I'll call for autopilot engaged and retract flaps as per normal takeoff.'

The briefing is completed and at 0622Z, the flight passes abeam Belfast. Using the PA, Don highlights some of the sights for the passengers. On the left side is Belfast, Belfast Lough, and beyond that, the Isle of Arran and the coast of Scotland. Travellers on the right side have a grand view of the breadth of Ireland. Ahead is the Isle of Man.

The radio crackles and it's Scottish control calling with a frequency change. Bob checks in with London air traffic control.

**Captain R/T:** 'London, it's Air Canada eight five six heavy level three seven oh.'

**London Control:** 'Air Canada eight five six, remain level three seven zero, standard routeing to Bovingdon, landing nine left.'

As predicted, the crew have been given the Bovingdon STAR which will take the flight over the Honiley VOR to WCO and on to BNN. The STAR chart advises pilots that they should plan to be at FL130 and 250kt by WCO, subject to ATC clearance. Details of the arrival routeing have already been entered into the FMC and with VNAV and

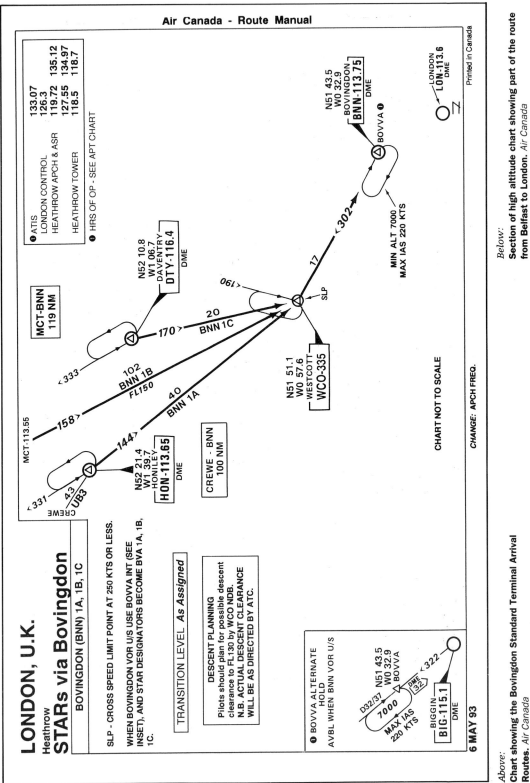

*Above:*
**Chart showing the Bovingdon Standard Terminal Arrival Routes.** *Air Canada*

*Below:*
**Section of high altitude chart showing part of the route from Belfast to London.** *Air Canada*

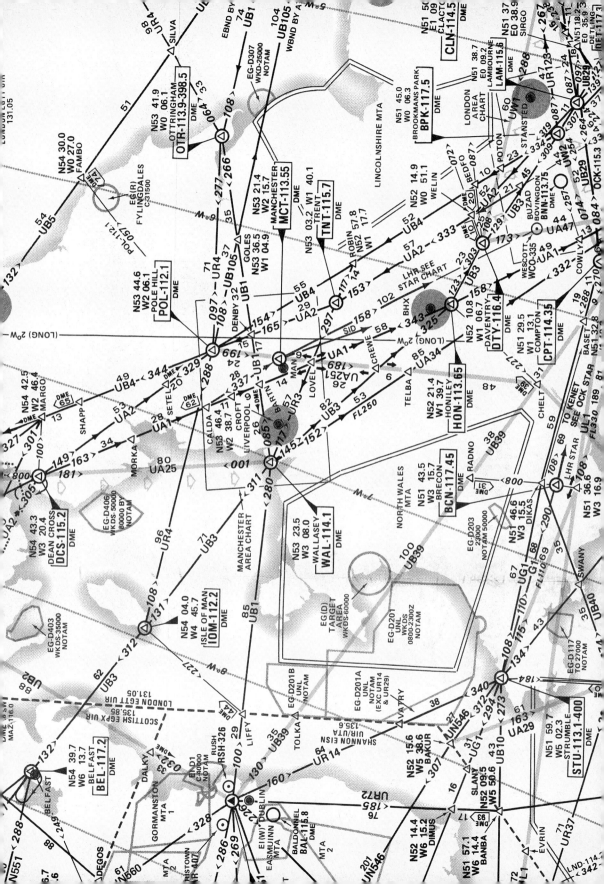

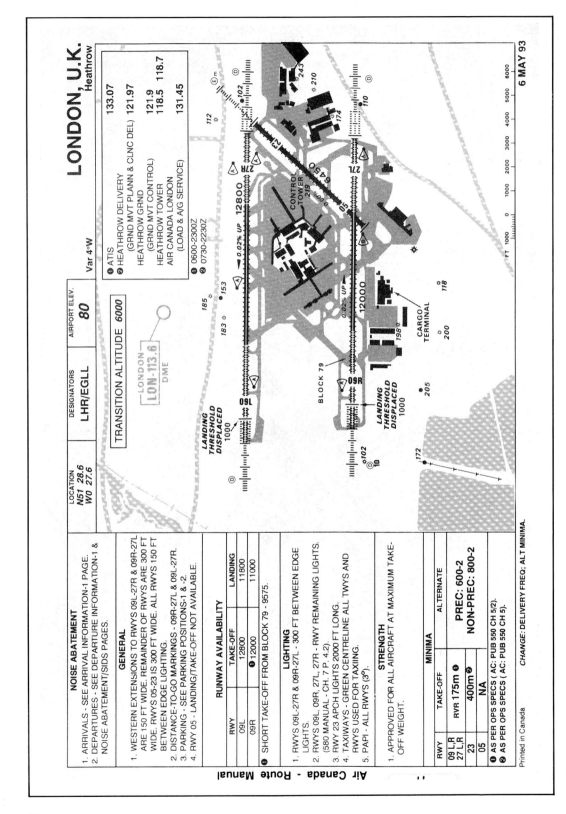

# LONDON, U.K.
Heathrow

| | | | |
|---|---|---|---|
| LOCATION N51 28.6 W0 27.6 | DESIGNATORS LHR/EGLL | AIRPORT ELEV. **80** | |

Var 4°W

TRANSITION ALTITUDE *6000*

LONDON
LON 113.6
DME

| | |
|---|---|
| ❶ ATIS | 133.07 |
| ❷ HEATHROW DELIVERY (GRND MVT PLANN & CLNC DEL) | 121.97 |
| HEATHROW GRND (GRND MVT CONTROL) | 121.9 |
| HEATHROW TOWER | 118.5  118.7 |
| AIR CANADA LONDON (LOAD & A/G SERVICE) | 131.45 |

❶ 0600-2300Z
❷ 0730-2230Z

6 MAY 93

*(chart labels: 27R, 27L, 09R, 09L, 10, CONTROL TOWER 219, CARGO TERMINAL, BLOCK 79, LANDING THRESHOLD DISPLACED 1000, 0.02% UP 12800, 0.02% UP 12000, 6450, 112, 153, 185, 183, 102, 172, 205, 200, 198, 118, 110, 174, 210, 243)*

FT 1000 0 1000 2000 3000 4000 5000 6000

---

**Air Canada - Route Manual**

## NOISE ABATEMENT
1. ARRIVALS - SEE ARRIVAL INFORMATION-1 PAGE.
2. DEPARTURES - SEE DEPARTURE INFORMATION-1 & NOISE ABATEMENT/SIDS PAGES.

### GENERAL
1. WESTERN EXTENSIONS TO RWYS 09L-27R & 09R-27L ARE 150 FT WIDE. REMAINDER OF RWYS ARE 300 FT WIDE. RWYS 05-23 IS 300 FT WIDE. ALL RWYS 150 FT BETWEEN EDGE LIGHTING.
2. DISTANCE-TO-GO MARKINGS - 09R-27L & 09L-27R.
3. PARKING - SEE PARKING POSITIONS-1 & -2.
4. RWY 05 - LANDING/TAKE-OFF NOT AVAILABLE.

### RUNWAY AVAILABILITY

| RWY | TAKE-OFF | LANDING |
|---|---|---|
| 09L | 12800 | 11800 |
| 09R | ❶ 12000 | 11000 |

❶ SHORT TAKE-OFF FROM BLOCK 79 - 9575.

### LIGHTING
1. RWYS 09L-27R & 09R-27L - 300 FT BETWEEN EDGE LIGHTS.
2. RWYS 09L, 09R, 27L, 27R - RWY REMAINING LIGHTS. (580 MANUAL - CH. 7 P. 4.2).
3. RWY 23 APCH LIGHTS 2000 FT LONG.
4. TAXIWAYS - GREEN CENTRELINE ALL TWYS AND RWYS USED FOR TAXIING.
5. PAPI - ALL RWYS (3°).

### STRENGTH
1. APPROVED FOR ALL AIRCRAFT AT MAXIMUM TAKE-OFF WEIGHT.

### MINIMA

| RWY | TAKE-OFF | ALTERNATE |
|---|---|---|
| 09 L,R 27 L,R | RVR 175m ❶ | PREC: 600-2 |
| 23 | 400m ❷ | NON-PREC: 800-2 |
| 05 | NA | |

❶ AS PER OPS SPECS ( AC: PUB 550 CH 5/2).
❷ AS PER OPS SPECS ( AC: PUB 550 CH 5).

Printed in Canada          *CHANGE: DELIVERY FREQ; ALT MINIMA.*

66

*Left:*
**Heathrow airport chart showing the layout of the runways, the terminals and the taxiways.** *Air Canada*

LNAV selected, the auto-pilot will fly the aircraft along the required flight profile.

The range of the Captain's ND is set to 160nm and at the top of the display, the symbol T/D appears on the track line, marking the point where the jet should start its descent into Heathrow. IOM is passed at 0630Z and the jet turns over the Irish Sea for the next waypoint which is WAL, a VOR at Wallasey, near Liverpool.

The cruise is nearly over and it's time for the crew to fasten their shoulder belts and clean up the flightdeck for the arrival ahead. The pace of chatter on the radio has picked up with the rush of early morning flights arriving at Heathrow. The crew run through the Pre-Descent checklist, checking Status and Recall on the EICAS; the approach briefing completed; ensuring that the MDA has been set; ADFs and ILS tuned for the approach; Vref 30, the final approach speed, is checked bugged on the airspeed tape at 145kt; and shoulder harnesses fastened. Heathrow ATIS is tuned on the right VHF to get the current airport weather and operating conditions.

**Heathrow ATIS:** 'Good morning, Heathrow information Golf. Zero six one five·weather: surface wind zero two zero at four knots, CAVOK. Temperature one five, dewpoint one zero, QNH one zero one niner millibars. Landing runway zero niner left, departure runway zero niner right. Pilots are asked to advise information Golf received when first contact with Heathrow.'

The details of the broadcast are noted on a small piece of paper and stuck on the centre console in clear view of both pilots. True to forecast, the sun has risen on a beautiful day in London.

At 0642Z, ATC responsibility for the flight changes once again and the Captain dials up the new frequency of 133.7.

**Captain R/T:** 'Air Canada eight five six heavy, level three seven oh, requesting descent.'
**London Control:** 'Air Canada eight five six heavy, descend now to Flight Level three five zero.'

As the Captain reads back the clearance, Don dials 35,000 in the altitude window and pushes the selector. After cruising smoothly for five and a half hours, it's time to start down. Minutes later, ATC is calling with lower.

**London Control:** 'Air Canada eight five six, descend to Flight Level three one zero.'

**Captain R/T:** 'Down to flight level three one oh, Air Canada eight five six.'

The altitude selector is wound down to the new altitude and as though commanded by an unseen hands, the throttles are retarded to flight idle by the auto-throttle. The jumbo becomes a big glider as it descends to the assigned altitude. The aircraft is dropping at 1,900ft/min and on the ND, a green arc crossing the track line indicates the new altitude will be reached in about 20nm.

**London Control:** 'Air Canada eight five six, make your heading now one three zero.'

The heading is selected and the aircraft gently banks to take up the new course.

**London Control:** 'Air Canada eight five six, descend to Flight Level two seven zero.'
**Captain R/T:** 'Flight Level two seven oh, Air Canada eight five six.'

Aware that the aircraft has started down, the passengers have begun their own preparations for the hustle and bustle of Heathrow and the city. They collect their personal belongings and check that important documents are at hand for ready scrutiny by immigration and customs personnel at the airport. Ahead is home, a vacation and for all, the end of a journey. It's like getting up in the morning and preparing for the day.

The aircraft is now descending at 3,400ft/min and the controller calls with clearance to FL230 and a right turn to 155°. The string of instructions continues non-stop as further clearances are given to 19,000ft and then down to 17,000. Initially Mach 0.86 is maintained in the descent but as the jet enters the denser air, the airspeed tape becomes the primary reference and 343kt is maintained by the auto-pilot. The crew has selected FL CH (Flight Level Change) rather than VNAV on the auto-pilot controls to keep pace with the flow of altitude changes coming from ATC.

The crew spot distant traffic at 9 o'clock that appears to be paralleling the flight's path, likely inbound to London as well. Air Canada 856 is cleared to 13,000 to be level at WCO, the Westcott NDB. The controller quickly calls back, changing that to 14,000ft before handing off the flight to the next London sector on 119.77.

Don reaches over beside the throttles and pulls the speed brake lever back. Five panels on the top of each wing raise up into the slipstream to reduce lift and create drag, allowing effective control of speed or descent rate. The flight spoilers also work automatically in conjunction with ailerons to provide additional roll control.

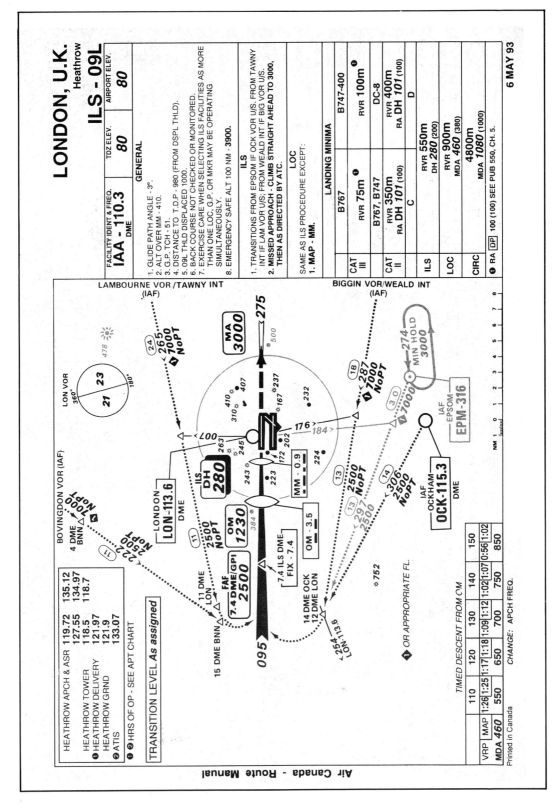

# LONDON, U.K.
## Heathrow
# ILS - 09L

| FACILITY IDENT & FREQ. | TDZ ELEV. | AIRPORT ELEV. |
|---|---|---|
| IAA - 110.3 DME | 80 | 80 |

## GENERAL

1. GLIDE PATH ANGLE - 3°.
2. ALT OVER MM - 410.
3. G.P. TCH - 51.
4. DISTANCE TO T.D.P. - 980 (FROM DSPL THLD).
5. 09L THLD DISPLACED 1000.
6. BACK COURSE NOT CHECKED OR MONITORED.
7. EXERCISE CARE WHEN SELECTING ILS FACILITIES AS MORE THAN ONE LOC, G.P. OR MKR MAY BE OPERATING SIMULTANEOUSLY.
8. EMERGENCY SAFE ALT 100 NM - 3900.

## ILS

1. TRANSITIONS FROM EPSOM IF OCK VOR U/S; FROM TAWNY INT IF LAM VOR U/S; FROM WEALD INT IF BIG VOR U/S.
2. MISSED APPROACH - CLIMB STRAIGHT AHEAD TO 3000, THEN AS DIRECTED BY ATC.

## LOC

SAME AS ILS PROCEDURE EXCEPT:
1. MAP - MM.

## LANDING MINIMA

| | B767 | B747-400 |
|---|---|---|
| CAT III | RVR 75m ❶ | RVR 100m ❶ |
| | B767, B747 | DC-8 |
| CAT II | RVR 350m RA DH 101 (100) | RVR 400m RA DH 101 (100) |
| | C | D |
| ILS | RVR 550m DH 280 (200) | |
| LOC | RVR 900m MDA 460 (380) | |
| CIRC | 4800m MDA 1080 (1000) | |

❶ RA DP 100 (100) SEE PUB 550, CH. 5.

HEATHROW APCH & ASR 119.72 135.12
HEATHROW TOWER 127.55 134.97
❶ HEATHROW DELIVERY 118.5 118.7
HEATHROW GRND 121.97 121.9
❷ ATIS 133.07
❶ ❷ HRS OF OP - SEE APT CHART

### TRANSITION LEVEL *As assigned*

LAMBOURNE VOR /TAWNY INT (IAF)
BIGGIN VOR/WEALD INT (IAF)
BOVINGDON VOR (IAF)
LON VOR

MA 3000
←275
095
MIN HOLD 3000
274
IAF EPSOM EPM-316
IAF OCKHAM OCK-115.3 DME
LONDON LON-113.6 DME
ILS DH 280
OM 1230
FAF 7.4 DME/GPI 2500
7.4 ILS DME FIX - 7.4
MM - 0.9
OM - 3.5
14 DME OCK 12 DME LON
15 DME BNN
11 DME LON
4 DME BNN △ 7000 NoPT
24 < 265 7000 NoPT
18 < 287 7000 NoPT
306 2500 NoPT
297 2500
2500 NoPT
2500 NoPT
L007
176
184
275
478
410
407
310
237
232
263
245
172
202
223
243
224
384
752
254 LON-113.6
222 2500 NoPT
3.0 7000
13
13
14
11
21 23

### TIMED DESCENT FROM OM

| | 110 | 120 | 130 | 140 | 150 |
|---|---|---|---|---|---|
| VRP MAP | 1:26 | 1:17 | 1:09 | 1:02 | 0:56 |
| | 1:25 | 1:18 | 1:12 | 1:07 | 1:02 |
| MDA 460 | 550 | 650 | 700 | 750 | 850 |

◆ OR APPROPRIATE FL.

CHANGE: APCH FREQ.

6 MAY 93

Printed in Canada

Air Canada - Route Manual

68

**London Control:** 'Air Canada eight five six, cleared direct to Bovingdon to hold.'

The ATC instructions are not unexpected by the crew. When traffic builds, the controller cannot simply have the aircraft stop in mid-air or pull over to the side of the road. So to meter the flow into the airport, aircraft are stacked in holds, flying a four-minute racetrack pattern at a designated spot, like over a VOR. Arriving at Heathrow during the busy morning rush usually means spending some time in a hold as ATC juggles the incoming aircraft.

The Captain calls up the HOLD page on the FMC, enters the outbound radial of the hold and the direction of the turns, in this case right. With this information, the FMS takes the aircraft's position and automatically figures out the best procedure to enter the hold. On ACARS, Bob calls Air Canada dispatch and asks to nominate Gatwick as the landing alternate rather than Glasgow.

Since Gatwick is much closer than Glasgow, the change reduces the fuel that must be held in reserve for a flight to the landing alternate. The net effect of this book-keeping exercise is extra holding time at BNN should it be required. The 747-400 burns about 6,800kg of fuel an hour in the hold and the FMC tells the pilots the flight can hold for 27min. Listening in on the chatter between the controller and other flights ahead though, it doesn't appear that the hold will be any longer than five or 10min.

Don stows the speed brakes and since the maximum speed in the hold is 220kt, less than the minimum clean speed, he calls for flaps to be extended. Reaching to the airspeed window on the auto-pilot control panel on the glareshield, he dials up 220kt in the speed window. The auto-throttle sets engine power for the new speed.

**First Officer:** 'Flap one please.'

The Captain moves the flap selector to the first notch. The extension of flaps unlocks the outboard ailerons which now move for added roll control at slower speeds; at high speeds they are 'locked out' by an electrically actuated mechanism. The aircraft is level at FL140 and pitched about five degrees nose up at the relatively slow speed of 219kt. It's 0700Z as the aircraft swings to the right to 302° for the outbound leg of the hold.

*Above:*
**A touch of speed brakes helps speed the descent.**

*Above right:*
**Approaching the hold. . .**

*Right:*
**. . . and in the hold. ND range is set to 20nm and shows a course from the VOR to the final approach course.**

The crew divide their attention between the instrumentation and the view outside. This is busy airspace and their vigilant look-out for other traffic is rewarded with several sightings, including 'Speedbird 27 Kilo', a 737 flying just below and ahead of them in the hold. At this lower altitude, the beauty of the English countryside is apparent.

**London Control:** 'Air Canada eight five six, descend to Flight Level one three zero.'

The new altitude is selected and Don calls 'fourteen for thirteen'. Further clearance down to FL120 comes just in time to save the crew from levelling.

**London Control:** 'Air Canada eight five six, continue descent to Flight Level one one zero and call

Heathrow approach on one one nine point seven two.'

119.72 is tuned.

**Captain R/T:** 'Air Canada eight five six in the hold Flight Level one two oh for one one oh.'
**Heathrow Approach:** 'Air Canada eight five six, continue in the Bovingdon hold and descend to one zero zero.'

The radio frequency is busy as the controller guides the flights out of the hold one by one and directs them on to the approach course. Air Canada 856 is turning for its third time round in the hold when ATC calls with clearance to 9,000 and a right turn to 240° for sequencing on to the final approach. As they leave the hold, it's time for the In-Range check. Landing lights are selected on, recall is checked, Vref and MDA both confirmed set, seatbelt sign on AUTO and auto-brakes set to 2 to provide moderate braking during roll-out.

The jet levels at 9,000ft, cruising at 223kt with the engine EPR at 1.02. Don calls for Flaps 5.

**Heathrow Approach:** 'Air Canada eight five six descend now to 4,000 feet. QNH is one zero one niner millibars.'

Landing lights are turned on.

The new altitude is selected and the current altimeter setting, set earlier from the ATIS, is confirmed on both PFDs and the standby altimeter.

**First Officer:** 'Flaps ten please.'
**Captain:** 'Flap ten selected.'
**Heathrow Approach:** 'Air Canada eight five six, contact radar one three five point one two.'

The frequency change is made and the crew are welcomed with yet another string of instructions.

**Heathrow Radar:** 'Air Canada eight five six left one eight zero, speed one eight zero.'

The aircraft turns to the assigned heading and the throttles retard slightly as the new speed is set in the airspeed window. Minutes later, ATC directs the flight on a southeasterly heading to intercept the localiser for 9 Left ILS.

**Heathrow Radar:** 'Air Canada eight five six, left one two zero. Call established zero nine left.'

The standy horizon has been set to approach mode and at the first indications that the ILS needles are 'alive', meaning that ILS signals are being received, the First Officer reaches to the glareshield and presses LOC, arming the auto-pilot to capture the localiser.

The first officer during the descent.

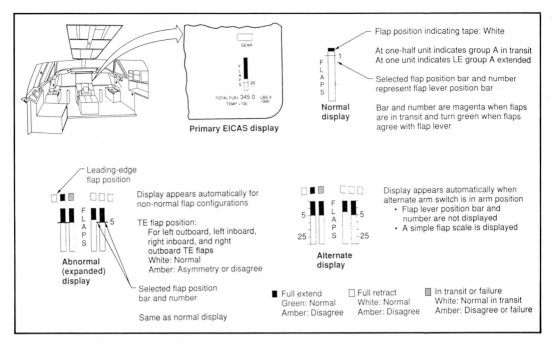

GEAR

F
L
A
P
S                    20

TOTAL FUEL 345.0    LBS x
TEMP +10c            1000

**Primary EICAS display**

Flap position indicating tape: White

At one-half unit indicates group A in transit
At one unit indicates LE group A extended

Selected flap position bar and number
represent flap lever position bar

F
L
A
P
S              1

**Normal
display**

Bar and number are magenta when flaps
are in transit and turn green when flaps
agree with flap lever

Leading-edge
flap position

Display appears automatically for
non-normal flap configurations

F
L
A
P
S              5

TE flap position:
   For left outboard, left inboard,
   right inboard, and right
   outboard TE flaps
   White: Normal
   Amber: Asymmetry or disagree

**Abnormal
(expanded)
display**

Selected flap position
bar and number

Same as normal display

Display appears automatically when
alternate arm switch is in arm position
   • Flap lever position bar and
     number are not displayed
   • A simple flap scale is displayed

F
L
A
P
S

5                    5

25                   25

**Alternate
display**

■ Full extend          □ Full retract          ▨ In transit or failure
   Green: Normal          White: Normal          White: Normal in transit
   Amber: Disagree        Amber: Disagree        Amber: Disagree or failure

*Above & Right:*
**The flap indications as shown on the upper EICAS and the
configuration of the leading and trailing edge flaps.** *Boeing*

The jet is still high as it nears the airport so Don deploys a touch of speed brake and dials up a descent rate on the vertical speed selector to increase the jet's descent. On each PFD, the localiser marker moves off the stop and toward the centre of the display as the jet banks to the left towards the runway. The localiser is intercepted about 12nm from the airport. The 737 spotted in the hold is heard on the same frequency ahead of the Air Canada flight on the approach.

**Heathrow Radar:** 'Air Canada eight five six descend on the ILS, speed of one sixty knots to the marker, call the tower one eighteen seven, good day.'

Don calls for the Before Landing check and that is the Captain's cue to move the gear handle to the DOWN position. A dull roar is heard from below as the gear doors open and the gear bogeys descend into the slipstream and lock into position, an action confirmed by a gear down and locked indication on the upper EICAS display. The gear doors swing shut again to reduce drag. Continuing with the checks, flaps are selected to 20° and the speed brake lever is moved to the armed position so the spoilers will automatically deploy when the wheels spin up on touchdown. The Captain recycles the no smoking sign several times, causing a chime to sound in the cabin to alert the flight attendants to take their seats for landing.

Now cleared for the approach, Don reaches again to the glareshield and presses APP to arm the auto-pilot to intercept the glideslope. This also arms the two remaining auto-pilots to engage at 1,500ft.

The Captain tunes 118.7 on the left VHF and checks in with the tower.

**Heathrow Tower:** 'Air Canada eight five six, report the outer marker for zero nine left.'

Until now, the flight had been controlled by the centre auto-pilot. But as the jet passes 1,500ft on the radio altimeter, the other two auto-pilots automatically engage. LAND 3 appears on each PFD, confirming that all three auto-pilots are in control. The auto-throttle remains engaged to fly the speed set in the airspeed window.

The speed is 161, Vref + 15, and the jet is descending at 950ft/min, established on the glideslope and the localiser. The crew are carefully monitoring the progress of the approach, their eyes roaming the instruments, taking in the altitude, the descent rate, the ILS signals and engine performance in quick scans before looking outside at the runway. Don has his hands resting lightly on the controls, ready to take over in the unlikely event of a failure.

Windsor Castle is visible below as the aircraft enters the final stages of the approach. Just over three miles back from the runway, the jet passes

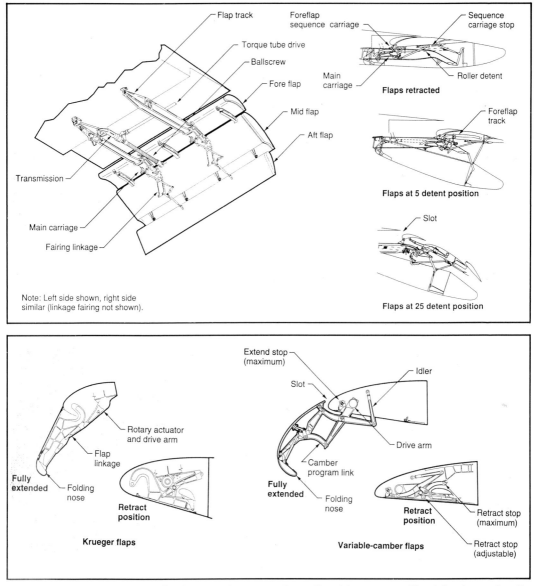

Note: Left side shown, right side similar (linkage fairing not shown).

**Flap track**, Foreflap sequence carriage, **Sequence carriage stop**, Torque tube drive, Ballscrew, Main carriage, Fore flap, Mid flap, Aft flap, **Flaps retracted**, Roller detent, **Foreflap track**, Transmission, **Flaps at 5 detent position**, Main carriage, Fairing linkage, **Slot**, **Flaps at 25 detent position**

Extend stop (maximum), Idler, Slot, Rotary actuator and drive arm, Drive arm, Flap linkage, Camber program link, **Fully extended** Folding nose, **Fully extended** Folding nose, **Retract position**, **Retract position**, Retract stop (maximum), Retract stop (adjustable), **Krueger flaps**, **Variable-camber flaps**

over the outer marker at 1,230ft. The Captain verifies that the jet is safely established on the glideslope and at Don's call, selects 30° flap. The flap system consists of four triple-slotted trailing edge flaps and the 28 leading edge flaps. When fully extended, the flaps increase the wing area by approximately 21% and the lift by about 90%. As the flaps extend, they change the wing geometry by first extending the chord and then increasing camber.

**Heathrow Tower:** 'Air Canada eight five six, after the landing seven three seven just touching down now cleared to land zero nine left. Surface winds are zero two zero at ten.'

The radio altimeter steadily ticks down the distance to the ground: 900 . . . 800 . . . 700ft.

At 500ft, the aircraft transitions to runway align. The auto-pilots stop crabbing the aircraft into the wind to compensate for drift and now align the jet with the runway centreline and drop the left wing slightly to compensate for the light crosswind, keeping the aircraft centred with rudder. The runway is visible ahead in the early morning haze and the British Airways 737 is seen rolling out. Passing 400ft, the Captain calls 'one hundred above' and then makes another call at 280ft.

**Captain:** 'Minimum. Runway in sight.'

**LOC is selected on the autoflight controls to intercept the localiser for Runway 9 Left.**

First Officer: 'Landing.'

At 100ft above ground level, the aircraft is just seconds from touchdown and the pilots make a quick check of the auto-land status to ensure all is okay. Across the top of each PFD, the auto-pilot status indications tell the crew that both the roll-out and flare modes are armed. Below 100ft, the aircraft is committed to land; the multiple auto-pilots will guard against any probable system failure and will safely land the jet.

Between 40 and 60ft, flare mode automatically activates and the throttles slowly retard. The nose pitches up slightly to flare the aircraft for landing. The Captain calls 30ft and both pilots confirm that the aircraft is flaring. If not, they would have to quickly flare the aircraft themselves.

**The controller has vectored the flight on to the final approach course above the glideslope. The First Officer dials up a descent rate on the auto-flight controls to speed the jet's descent to intercept the ILS.**

Five feet above the runway, roll-out mode activates ensuring that the auto-pilots will track within five feet of the runway centreline after touchdown.

A loud rumble is heard from below as the 16 main wheels touch down. The spoilers immediately deploy to reduce lift and the nosewheel gently lowers on to the runway. The throttles have retarded automatically to idle and Don calls for reverse thrust. Bob pulls the throttles back past

the idle position to position the blocker doors. On each engine, a section of cowling slides aft to block the flow of fan exhaust and redirect it forward to slow the aircraft. After checking the upper EICAS display to ensure reverse thrust has deployed on each engine, Bob calls 'Operating'. Don takes over the throttles and a loud roar is heard as he eases the levers back to spool up the engines. The deceleration is brisk as auto-brakes and reverse thrust combine to slow the jet. During roll-out, Bob calls out the speeds.

**Captain:** 'One hundred . . . eighty . . . sixty. . . .'

Don begins reducing the reverse thrust at 100kt and returns the throttles to the idle position by 60kt to avoid ingesting dirt or debris into the engines.

The jet slows to taxying speed and the loud whoop, whoop, whoop of an alarm fills the cockpit as the Captain cancels the auto-pilot and takes control. If the auto-pilot was inadvertently left on, it would continue to track within 5ft of the centreline, fighting the efforts of the pilot to taxi the jet off the runway.

**Heathrow Tower:** 'Air Canada eight five six, right turn there. Contact ground on one two one decimal nine.'

*Top:*
**The auto-brake selector.**

*Above:*
**2.7 miles out. The jet is at 980ft (880ft above ground as shown by the radio altimeter read-out) flying at 151kt. Three auto-pilots are in control as confirmed by the LAND 3 indication. Above that, ROLLOUT and FLARE modes are shown as armed.**

*Right:*
**Short final. . .**

Being careful not to take the turn too fast, Bob steers the jet off the runway on to the next taxiway using the nosewheel tiller located on the sidewall. When passing through 10,000ft, ACARS automatically sent a message to the airline office's at Heathrow with the flight's estimated arrival time at the gate. This in turn prompted a return message with the flight's assigned gate so the crew know in advance where they are taxying to.

**First Officer R/T:** 'London ground, it's Air Canada eight five six cleared the active.'
**Heathrow Ground:** 'Air Canada eight five six, right turn on the outer taxiway for Mike two six.'

As the jet enters the taxiway, Don runs through the After Landing check: landing and strobe lights are turned off; the auto-throttle selected to off; radar is checked off; spoilers and flaps retracted; the stabiliser trim set to the neutral setting of six units; the auto-brakes knob is turned to OFF. He reaches to the overhead panel and turns on the APU as well as the two APU generators so electrical power is available to the aircraft once the engines have been shut down. On the Captain's command, the fuel cocks for Engines 2 and 3 are turned off, shutting down the engines to save fuel.

The aircraft is going to gate Mike 26 at Terminal 3, which is just a short taxi away. As the jet taxies on to the tarmac surrounding the terminal,

*Top left:*
**. . . over the numbers.**

*Bottom left:*
**Touchdown! The throttles are eased back to deploy reverse thrust and help slow the jet.**

the groundcrew can be seen busily working around the gate, preparing a variety of equipment to unload and service the aircraft once it has docked. With a practised touch, Bob steers the jet on to the yellow line leading to the gate. A visual aid attached to the terminal building helps guide pilots as they approach the terminal. The aid displays two green bars of light when the jet is centred. If the aircraft moves to one side or the other, the corresponding bar turns red.

The jet eases to a stop at the gate. The parking brake is set and the remaining two engines are

*Right:*
**Taxying at Heathrow.**

*Below:*
**The Captain steers the jet across the ramp to the gate.**

*Below right:*
**The upper EICAS display after landing. Note that Engines 2 and 3 have been shut down.**

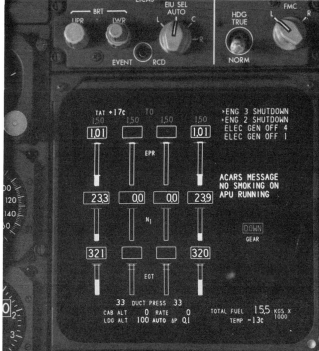

The groundcrew wait at Mike 26 to greet Air Canada 856.

shut down. It's 0721Z. Air Canada 856 is in London after a flight of 6hr 3min, and a chock-to-chock time of 6hr 24min. The upper EICAS shows 15,500kg of fuel remaining, slightly less than forecast but still 2,000kg above the minimum required reserves. Total fuel burn for the flight was 64,700kg.

The crew run through the shutdown checks, turning off the hydraulic pumps, fuel pumps, emergency lights, anti-ice, window heat and aft cargo heat. Any snags from the flight are noted in the journey logbook to alert ground technicians as well as the incoming crew.

The crew bus awaits below on the tarmac, ready to take the pilots and cabin crew through customs and immigration and then on to their downtown hotel. Many in the crew will grab a few hours' sleep and then get up in the afternoon for a walk, some shopping or seeing some of the sights. They will usually meet for an early supper before turning in for the night.

Tomorrow morning, the crew will be back at Heathrow to do it all over again, this time as Air Canada Flight 857, the return flight to Toronto.

## Boeing 747-400 Combi Technical Data

| | |
|---|---|
| Wingspan: | 211ft 5in (64.4m) |
| Overall Length: | 231ft 10in (70.6m) |
| Tail Height: | 63ft 5in (19.3m) |
| Body Width: | 20ft 1in (6.1m) |
| Maximum Take-off Weight: | 800,000lb (362,900kg) to 870,000lb (394,630kg) |
| Passengers: | 277 (16 First, 50 Business, 211 Economy. Numbers can vary depending on configuration.) |
| Cargo: | 6,085cu ft of cargo space on lower deck and room for seven pallets on main deck |
| Engines: | Four Pratt & Whitney 4056 turbofans rated at 56,000lb (25,400kg) each |
| Fuel Capacity: | 57,285 US gal (216,850 litres) |
| Range: | 6,590nm |

*Above:*
**Safely at the gate. The aircraft is quickly unloaded.**

*Overleaf:*
**A collection of tails. Once parked, a post is placed under the tail to ensure the jet stays level. Since the passengers leave the aircraft before the cargo in the aft compartments and main deck is unloaded, the jet becomes tail heavy. Without the pole, the jet's nose could rise off the ground.**

*Left:*
**There's no escape from the paperwork. The aircraft journey log is filled out.**